How to
Find the Champion
within Themselves

How to Help Children Find the Champion within Themselves

David Hemery

Published by BBC Active, an imprint of Educational Publishers LLP, part of the
Pearson Education Group, Edinburgh Gate, Harlow, Essex CM20 2JE, England

First published 2005.
15 14 13
Imp 10 9 8 7 6 5

ISBN: 978 0 563 51968 3

Commissioning editor: Emma Shackleton
Edited by: Content Consultants
Project editor: Sarah Sutton
Text designer: Martin Hendry
Cover designer: Annette Peppis
Cartoons and cover illustration: David Lewi
Production controller: Man Fai Lau
Set in Monotype Ehrhardt and Univers Ultra Condensed
Printed and bound in China (SWTC/05)

Contents

Preface

'As coaches, we are Guardians of the Flame – the flame being the enthusiasm in our performers.'

Bruce Tulloh, Olympic Coach

If you have opened this book, it probably means that you have the interest and capability to make a difference to the life of at least one young person. My intent is to help adults to become more effective at unlocking the magic that sits inside every individual. I have a belief that there is a spark of greatness in everyone. Each person has something unique and special within. *How to Help Children Find the Champion within Themselves* illustrates how we may help young people to find their greatness, to believe in themselves and recognise that they have something special to contribute to this world, just as we all have.

The opening quote to this preface comes from a conversation between Bruce Tulloh, a highly respected distance-running coach, and the coach of a talented young female javelin thrower who was about to leave school. The javelin coach had asked his student whether she would continue throwing javelin in college competition. She had replied, 'No way!' On asking, 'Why not?' he was told, 'You were interested only in seeing how far you could get me to throw. You weren't interested in me!' The coach had been shattered by her comment. Bruce said to him, 'As coaches, we are Guardians of the Flame – the flame being the enthusiasm in our performers.' I am extremely grateful to Bruce for allowing me to use his words to illustrate the main theme throughout this book.

We need to recognise that in our desire to help our young people, our emphasis on telling them what we think and what they should do, before asking for their opinion, probably inhibits their self-development and self-confidence. My aim is to show how we can each be a 'Guardian of the Flame' that exists within every child, as well as in us.

■ My 'ah ha!' moment

In 1987 I was introduced to Richard Evans, an engineer who had made his fortune through the development of the project-management software, Artemis. He took time to put himself on a personal development course and discovered a life-transforming 'ah ha!' moment. Early on in his career, he understood that his autocratic, controlling style needed modification. Largely his success had come through his drive and considerable intellect, but those alone were not sufficient for business. He had the insight to recognise that young people were changing. He could not recruit and motivate bright performers without moving towards a more consultative style. Eventually he sold his business, trained as a counsellor, and put some of his money into trust. With this he started sponsoring parenting courses. When he found that virtually no fathers came, he asked my colleague, motor racing champion John Whitmore, how he might reach the male half of our population. John pointed out that the vast majority of sport coaches are male and that they relate with millions of young people. Richard enjoyed sport, but shared that his priority intent was not to generate more gold medals; however, if a course addressed how sport coaches could use questioning to develop young people, he would agree to support our work to develop and run courses.

John knew that I had been in education and had a passion for unlocking potential in young people. Together with Olympic hockey player and gold medal coach David Whitaker, we worked with the National Coaching Foundation to bring this concept into the training of sports coaches. What percentage of coaches work for their living and coach in the evenings and at weekends? Most! So what do you think happened? Within weeks we had participants saying, 'This will be great for unlocking potential on the sports field but we could really use this at work. Would you come and speak with our human resource managers?' Several months later our main work was within business. Our company, Performance Consultants, was established and, as they say, the rest is history. Since 1987 we have travelled the UK and abroad, sharing insights and running courses, in what became known as 'coaching' in management. John Whitmore's book *Coaching for Performance* became the bible of coaching philosophy and skills.

Business used the term 'coaching' to distinguish 'asking and listening' from the highly autocratic 'telling/pushing' style that was quite effective while things were changing slowly. The term 'coaching' was not our choice, as we knew that most sport coaching was generally by instructors and at times very autocratic.

Changes in business and technology started to accelerate. One person, or the few, at the top of an organisation could not effectively manage everything necessary to keep up with these changes. They had to find a way to unlock the previously untapped potential in others in their companies. Coaching fitted that demand perfectly.

In the context of coaching young people, parameters need to be set. The implication of 'asking' is that we are requesting that our young people act responsibly. We are treating them as adults and would value responses that reflect that treatment. It would be sensible to state our intent and expectations, especially if flippant answers are expected or received. Humour is a great asset and this needs to be combined with a level of commitment that will do justice to young people and their work.

My hope is that sufficient numbers begin to generate true awareness and responsibility and thereby bring about a shift in humanity's capability to build a world in which love outweighs fear; where challenge and support promotes excellence; where tolerance and compassion are the norm; and where creativity and positive intent continually generate new possibilities.

Introduction

■ Why did I want to write this?

My biggest reason for writing this book is that I care passionately that we modify how we communicate, in order to better develop the potential in our young people. I hope that this text will convey the passion I feel for changing how we primarily relate with and involve our young people. I also hope that something in this text will awaken and inspire parents, grandparents, coaches, teachers and leaders, to make us want to enhance our communication and relationship skills.

Most of us will have had a spectrum of experiences in our life. I feel fortunate to have had a wider spectrum than most and that has greatly helped me to appreciate more of what is needed to fulfil our potential. I recognise the primarily negative impact of criticism and the generally positive effect of high support and challenge. When I moved from Britain to the USA, aged twelve, I was very small for my age. The sports of baseball or basketball were new to me. I experienced the ignominy of being left until last when teams were being chosen by the two best players, and having them argue over who would be forced to have me on their team. Neither wanted such a pathetic liability. This confidence–deflating process is still used today. Do adults not recognise the potentially negative effect of being labelled 'useless'?

I moved on from that experiece to learn what it takes to become an Olympic champion and world record holder. This book has more to do with motivating the young person's spirit, stimulating their keenness to learn and to overcome barriers, and constantly to acknowledge their self-improvement, than placing total emphasis on finishing first.

I also know what it feels like to be considered dumb. I had huge difficulty learning how to read (mild dyslexia was not in any parent's or teacher's understanding when I was a child) and I overheard snide remarks between teachers, such as, 'If you have all day, try listening to David Hemery read.' Perhaps the need to prove myself in that area was what led me to complete four degrees at Boston University, Oxford and Harvard, although I am sure that the choice of my doctoral thesis: 'What makes a Champion' came from my huge interest in finding out what enables people to achieve more of their potential.

■ Coaching – asking effective questions

For more than a dozen years I have been working with managers and leaders in business to enhance their questioning and listening skills. They wanted to distinguish their 'telling' style from an emphasis on questioning, so they chose the term 'coaching'. This term presents problems because most people associate coaching with sport and also most sport coaches are primarily 'instructors'. For the sake of this text I have avoided using the term coaching, and have spoken about the power of effective questioning and attentive listening. Having said that, it can be helpful if we can see ourselves as coaches of our young people, willing to shift our own emphasis from voicing our opinions first, to asking for their views first.

This book illustrates how to ask questions that are likely to promote empowerment. Questioning effectively and listening attentively can help to move our young people's authority from external (mostly us) to internal (themselves). If our questions generate more of their awareness and self-responsibility, the likely result is an increase in our young people's self-belief. Lack of self-belief, low self-confidence, doubts and fears inhibit potential. Shifting our emphasis from telling to asking is simple to understand, yet much more difficult to ingrain.

Effective questions can have extraordinary and positive results. Using questions does not mean we should stop making our contributions by telling, but, if we ask first, we generate a significant difference in the minds and hearts of our young people. Probably most of us believe that we do have the best interests of our young people in mind. That may be true, but most of our role models have been our own parents, grandparents, teachers and coaches, who usually will have led our thinking by telling, rarely asking questions that were effective in making us think or take real responsibility for our own growth and development. How many of us have, at times, noticed that we are acting or sounding like our parents? It is a lot easier just to follow what we have previously experienced. Asking ourselves to try something different may sound easy, but changing the habits of a lifetime is never easy. We may find initially that it is hard even to find the ideal wording for an effective question.

Asking a question that aims to generate awareness and responsibility in a young person may sound simple. However, it is rarely done well. It was not covered during my time of teacher-training, and it came as a great shock to realise that I might have been dulling the flame/enthusiasm in my young people. As a parent, a coach and a teacher, I had given guidance, made suggestions and followed my agenda of 'trying to be helpful'. I had taken most of the responsibility for the thinking for young people and by doing this had failed to grow their self-thought, self-awareness, self-responsibility and therefore their self-belief. Yet, on reflection, these were all the things I had wanted to have happen within these young people.

To make sure that we are asking appropriate and effective questions of young people, we may usefully reflect on a few questions of our own:

■ What is our intent?

■ Whose agenda are we on – theirs or ours?

■ Can we discover their wishes before sharing ours?

■ How do we find an acceptable way forward for them and us?

■ Are we initiating their greater self-awareness through our questions?

■ Are we prompting the young person's choice to take responsibility?

I have no doubt that most of us, at some time, will have asked questions and listened in a way that made our young people think for themselves. However, have we recognised the huge potential benefits? Here are a few:

■ Happier, more empowered young people, who feel heard and valued.

■ Their buy-in and commitment to ideas generated with hearts and minds engaged.

■ Greater awareness, responsibility and self-belief generated.

■ Greater focus on the issue at hand – thereby enhanced use of time; accelerated personal learning and development.

■ More creative solutions and potential developed for the issue at hand.

■ Higher-quality relationships between the young people and ourselves.

■ Our caring is expressed by giving young people higher-quality time and attention.

■ Increased mutual trust through more openness and sharing of ideas, feelings and dreams.

If these are the results, can we afford not to take our communication more seriously?

I have divided the book into three sections, aimed at the parent, the teacher and the coach; each is designed to show common scenarios from different perspectives and includes key learning points for action. For ease of reference, positively phrased questions are marked: ■.

Getting the basics right

Whose agenda is it?

Every young person has their own agenda, whether or not it is clear to us, or to them. With some reflection, most of us can become aware of our own agenda or intent. Many of us would like to help our young people. We would also like to see them develop and get the best out of themselves. With this as our agenda, we are going to be very tempted to steer, guide, suggest, tell, persuade and sometimes push young people. If we do this, we may well generate a push back.

If we push for *our* aims, interests and values without listening to theirs, there is a good chance that we will meet resistance or possibly turn them off. If it is not in their interest to co-operate, how can we expect them to want to co-operate? We are likely to see a general lowering of their motivation and performance.

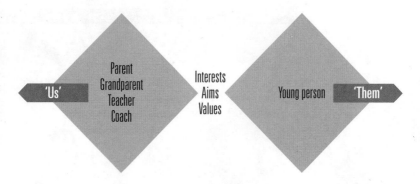

However, if we seek to find what engages the hearts and minds of our young people, and if we are open and flexible, we will get more from them, and our communication and relationship will be enhanced.

The following has been referred to as a dance because it is our choice consciously to move from one side to the other, as the situation, individual or team-needs demand. Being stuck on one side or the other is unhelpful for our young people and us.

THE TELLING AND ASKING DANCE

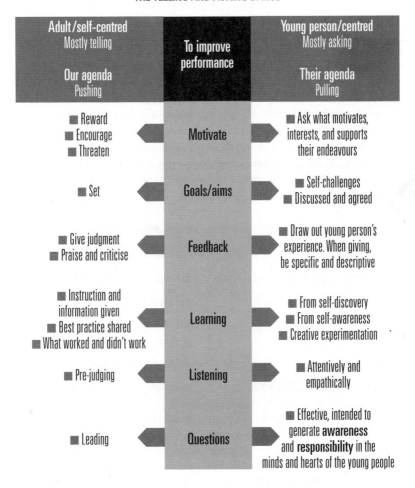

Adult/self-centred Mostly telling Our agenda Pushing	To improve performance	Young person/centred Mostly asking Their agenda Pulling
■ Reward ■ Encourage ■ Threaten	Motivate	■ Ask what motivates, interests, and supports their endeavours
■ Set	Goals/aims	■ Self-challenges ■ Discussed and agreed
■ Give judgment ■ Praise and criticise	Feedback	■ Draw out young person's experience. When giving, be specific and descriptive
■ Instruction and information given ■ Best practice shared ■ What worked and didn't work	Learning	■ From self-discovery ■ From self-awareness ■ Creative experimentation
■ Pre-judging	Listening	■ Attentively and empathically
■ Leading	Questions	■ Effective, intended to generate **awareness** and **responsibility** in the minds and hearts of the young people

■ The push-you, pull-you technique

How often do we hear young people being pushed, perhaps yelled at from a sideline, or being told what to do or not do, by parents, grandparents, teachers or coaches? These suggestions and directives may not be in the direction that is best for the individual concerned.

A great parallel about pushing and pulling can be found in architecture. Donald Insall, the architect who restored Windsor Castle after the 1998 fire, said that if an arch supported by two pillars is in danger of collapse, because one or both pillars are bowing outwards, a tie that pulls the pillars together is much more effective than massive buttresses pushing from the outside. What he added was hugely significant in its parallel with the effect on humans. He said that the effect of the tie is that the pillars pull themselves into alignment. When the pillars are pushed, often the forces are not in exactly the right direction.

Problems created by only telling (push)	Problems of only asking questions (pull)
■ Adult stuck with all the problems	■ We frustrate genuine information seeker
■ Limited to our knowledge and ideas	■ We have to think before we speak!
■ We could stifle creativity	■ It takes longer in the short term
■ One way, not a team	■ We never share our opinion
■ We could lose respect — seen as dictator	■ We don't share our experiences
■ We may well generate dependence	■ We never give heartfelt praise

We have probably all heard recommendations or warnings from others who think they know what we should or should not do, and often we do not feel comfortable with their advice. It feels as if we are being misdirected or pushed in *their* chosen direction. How much better it can feel if someone asks us what we think would be the best direction for ourselves. It does not prevent us asking for their advice or ideas. It simply means that their asking is likely to prompt us to look at determining our own future. Life is about choices, and effective questions help to prompt wiser decision-making.

▪ Working together responsively – aligning our aims, interests and values

Really getting to know someone's aims, interests and values will not happen without an open and meaningful discussion. To reach significant agreement may require some movement by both parties. We all have a certain amount of effort and spirit that we choose to give or withhold. This is our **discretionary effort** (illustrated below by the darker-shaded area).

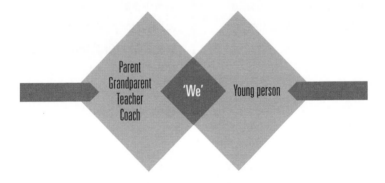

Check it from your own experience. What has been your reaction when a young person with great talent or exceptional needs has asked if you would be willing to work with them? If our interest and/or compassion have been fired, we may well react with some excitement to the possibilities and responsibilities, the value, the pressures, the learning opportunities and glow that could come from success. We may start to think about strategies and programmes and possibilities. Why do we do this unpaid review work? We do it because we can understand the personal benefit in it for us, as well as for our young person.

And, from their side, if we give them focused attention and we shift a bit towards what they are interested in doing, our young people will be far more likely to co-operate and work with us on aspects that they have not been so keen to advance before. It means that, by our giving time and interest, we may generate more of the effort that they have at their discretion. It is in both of our interests and generates a win–win situation.

Some benefits of telling	Some benefits of asking
■ We don't have to reinvent the wheel	■ Young people learn responsibility
■ We share best practice	■ We unlock their ideas and motivation
■ Everyone values positive encouragement	■ They and we are involved and aligned
■ We all need recognition and support	■ Potential for quality use of time
■ It's quicker to tell (in the short term)	■ Higher-quality relationships
	■ Generates self-responsibility and awareness
	■ More trust generated
	■ Happier young people
	■ Enhanced self-belief

2

Family
matters

First things first

■ Being nearest and dearest: 'knowing best'

Anyone who is bringing up a child will recognise that all the manuals in the world cannot prepare us adequately. Every child is different, and those of us who have more than one are usually astonished at how different they are, since they share some of the same genes and are living in the same environment. Given this diversity, I hope that some of the suggested 'questioning' strategies will help us to advance each child on their unique path; to help them to learn and develop with enthusiasm, in positive directions.

Sometimes we feel we know our children so well that we make incorrect assumptions about how they feel, what they want and what is good for them, without asking their opinion. We may often find ourselves speaking to them in a way we don't speak to other people, being demanding, dictatorial; perhaps we find we are projecting our feelings on to them – of anxiety for their safety, for example; sometimes we misinterpret our children's feelings and behaviour.

Who's doing the thinking here? And whose agenda is being voiced? Is the adult trying to help? Or exercising power and control?

How many of us assume that we know best? How often do we drive our ideas, ignore involvement and stifle the development of our young people's creativity or thought?

It is more effective to ask for their ideas first, *before* we tell them our views. Keep questions simple, to enable you *both* to focus on what you are trying to achieve. Just ask:

- ■ 'What are your ideas?'

- ■ 'What could you do?'

- ■ ''What do you want to happen?'

■ Nurturing the spark

Enthusiasm is very precious.

Self-belief can be quite fragile.

Hope and aspiration are invaluable, if young people are to fulfil their potential.

We need to be really careful to respond in a way that supports enthusiasm as well as having realism, for example:

■ 'That is a great challenge. It would take lots of work. How interested are you in learning more?'

■ Negotiating boundaries

We know what we would like them to do, but what is our motivation? Could the need to influence and control be clouding our thinking?

One of our gifts to young people is to establish boundaries or limits for them and then to allow them to experiment with their way of dealing with life. These boundaries can be negotiated and might include time, behaviour, language, or any other issue that contributes to their life choices.

If we have real concerns about their choices, we can ask the young person to consider the consequences of their actions. Once they are aware, they then have their own decisions to make.

Communication

■ Watch out for negative language

To make sense of Grandad's command, the young girl must think about spilling the soup, which probably makes that the more likely outcome! We must keep our language positive, and state what we want rather than what we do not want.

■ 'Don't spill it!' could become, 'Hold it carefully – it's very full.'

■ 'Don't look down!' could become, 'Keep looking up.'

■ 'Don't forget it!' could become, 'How will you remember it?'

■ Speaking 'for' them

What does speaking for our young people do for their development, or for their sense of self-worth, confidence or independence?

We may need to learn to be comfortable with silence, while our young person is given time to think and speak.

■ Getting the message across

How many of us get turned off by repeatedly being told?

Research shows that 'telling' is the least effective style of communication to enable someone to recall what has been said. In the long term, we remember about 10 per cent of what we are told.

Telling does not require the young person to engage their own brain or to take ownership of what they are being told.

The following few questions may get the young person more involved and action-focused:

- 'Where would you want to store your clothes?'

- 'How long would it take you to tidy your room?'

- 'When would you be willing to tidy your room?'

If our young people are leaving their things all over the place, an awareness-raising question is:

- 'What effect do you think it has on us to have your things all over our space?'

A challenge to parents is, 'Whose problem is it?' If he or she is not leaving things around the house, how much does it matter that his or her space is untidy?

■ Getting to the point

If we decide to try asking more questions but steer our young people towards following our own agenda, we can cause them massive frustration. They would really prefer us to tell them what we want, need or would like to have.

Here are a few 'leading questions':

'Don't you think you could be doing something more useful right now?'

'Is that really the most important thing for you to be doing right now?

'Will you feel like helping me later?'

Most people would rather hear a direct statement:

■ 'I would be really grateful for a hand with the drying up.'

■ Challenging behaviour

Sometimes we may need to challenge young people's behaviour. However, we may need to look first at our own style of communication, as it may have prompted the young person's reaction.

We cannot assume that their way of expressing themselves will always be acceptable or comfortable for us, when it is the young person's time to learn appropriate assertiveness.

Our challenge is to generate their choice to communicate more effectively and acceptably. For example, we state the negative effect or impact that it had on us, then ask them how they might express themselves in a more constructive way.

■ Paying attention

No one said that parenting was easy.

This picture says: 'Oh, do whatever you want… (as long as you don't bother me!).'

It takes patience and energy always to concentrate and answer questions, comments, frustrations or requests.

Having eye contact can let young people know that we are paying attention.

■ Learning to listen

Really listening is one of the most underrated of human activities. Giving someone our full attention can do several things: it can say, 'I value you and what you have to say'; it can enhance the speaker's own focus on what they are trying to express; it can validate their opinion; it can remove the 'them' and 'us' barrier; it can be seen as a gift because time is precious.

How well do we to listen to a young person's intent, rather than the content? We may need to check that we have understood correctly by asking them if what we heard matches their intent.

Also, how often do we listen well enough to be able to ask an effective follow-on question that is on the young person's agenda?

Of course, it may be appropriate to challenge the speaker's assertion – 'You never listen!' Sometimes people overstate in order to make a point. An appropriate response might be a gentle:

■ 'Do you really mean never?'

If we listen with our hearts, noticing young people's emotions, their volume, their tone, their eyes, their body movement, as well as the information coming from their words, we can gain a much richer understanding of what they are expressing.

■ Learn to listen: bullying

These days we hear a lot about the high number of young people who are bullied. As someone who experienced bullying as a child, I am conscious that the first response of many children would be to deny that they are being bullied.

Adults often ask closed questions, such as, 'Is everything okay?' The reflex answer is usually, 'Yes!' when actually it is not.

If our intuition tells us that a child may be hiding something, we could ask a question, such as:

■ 'If everything wasn't okay, what would you do?'

■ 'Who would you talk to?'

■ 'What might happen if you told someone about a bullying situation?'

■ 'What's the worst that could happen if you told someone?'

■ 'What's the likelihood of that outcome?'

■ 'If a friend of yours were in trouble or being bullied, what would you recommend that they did?'

Even if we ask an open question, the young person may say that they don't want to talk right now. We do need to honour their right to privacy, and we need also to provide them with opportunities to share problems and get help if it is needed.

Recognising independence

■ Projecting our fears

How often do we project our anxieties and fears onto young people?

What we say may raise a focus in the young person's mind that can create tension and bring about fear.

Instead of 'Get down! You'll fall!!' an alternative comment here might be:

■ 'That is amazing balance. Can you show me how you get down from there?'

The comment encourages the child to demonstrate prowess by returning (safely) to the ground.

■ Generating dependence?

How much does our taking responsible actions deny our young people their own growth and development?

Do we sometimes do so much of the thinking and providing for our young people that they become too dependent or complacent?

In the words of bestselling writer David McNally, 'even eagles need a push', to leave the comfort of the nest.

■ Understanding consequences

'Why did you do that?' would probably be followed by a labelling, such as: 'You idiot!'

Frequently, 'why' is not a helpful way to begin a question. Often the young person does not know why they did something, nor why a result turned out a particular way.

More helpful questions are those that can be answered from the young person's experience. And the vast majority of effective questions begin with 'What...'

■ 'What did you intend to do?'

■ 'What can you learn from this?'

■ 'What would you do differently next time?'

(And, in this case, 'Please will you help stack these up again?!')

■ Getting it right

This mum has neatly avoided being drawn into the siblings' argument and perhaps having to take sides. However, her reply is not one of abdication, as her statement generates responsibility in the two young people, and lets them know that she believes in their capability for more mature problem-solving.

Points of view

■ Learning to compromise

Parents and children may have frequent and significant disagreements. Both sides can be vociferous in expressing their differences in perception and values.

One insight is that each party is asking the other to change. The challenge is to find acceptable compromise on both their parts.

Einstein said, 'We cannot solve problems at the same level that we created them.'

This means that we must either go deeper, or we need to detach ourselves and view the problem from a different perspective or vantage point.

One option is to place ourselves in the other person's position and see what they are experiencing, both in the situation and with us. Another is to imagine that you are coming to the issue from outside and view the situation as a neutral wise observer.

■ Conflict of interest

Time is an issue for many of us.

Our Dad's reply, above, needs to acknowledge his daughter's interest and let her know his constraints. For example:

■ 'I know that you'd like me to look at it now, but I have a taxi waiting and don't have the time to do it justice at the moment. I'd love to see it later. Can you keep it safe until tomorrow night?'

■ Never enough

By picking on what someone has done wrong, we may generate one of the classic feelings caused by parents: 'I can never be good enough!'

How could we celebrate what is best in their efforts? By saying, for example:

■ 'Well done! How do you feel about that?'

■ Stealing their say

Sometimes great questions get ruined by asking multiple, leading or follow-on questions. We are sometimes so eager to help, that we start thinking for our young people. An effective, thought-provoking question is:

■ 'What do you really want to do?'

If we ask such a question, we may need to feel comfortable with silence, as our young person may need thinking time.

Our gift to them is to resist the urge to fill the silence while they think through their thoughts and wishes. We need also to learn to feel comfortable with not knowing where a conversation may go.

■ Curiosity

How can we avoid killing off natural curiosity?

Questions can be challenging – we may not know all the answers, we may be feeling emotionally stressed, we may not have the time to do justice to the young person's inquiry.

How can we balance giving them answers with asking them where else they might find out the information? It may be that we agree a time when we will give them our full attention. If we believe that the young person is simply being lazy in their thinking, we could ask:

■ 'What would you do if I weren't here?'

■ Prior involvement can save a lot of aggravation

There are several possible reolutions to this scenario. We can:

■ Ask what the young person would like to eat – before the meal (and, if need be, negotiate).

■ Let them take the amount that they feel comfortable finishing (and if need be, hold them to that).

■ Check that they do not fill themselves with crisps and sweets between meals.

■ Ask them what is really going on in their refusal to eat. It could be a cry for attention or it may be just that the child does not like that food and never has liked it.

Losing it!

■ Keeping your ambition in check

How many parents, who did not quite make it in sport or other areas of their lives, try to make their children fulfil their adult need to achieve?

■ Recognising pain

There may be occasions when we are less than fearful for our children, when our desire to encourage toughness and determination means we ignore what's going on for them. Is it our embarrassment or frustration that makes us lack empathy in the type of situation illustrated here?

Useful questions to ask a young person in discomfort are:

■ 'On a scale of 1–10 how much is this hurting/bothering you?'

■ 'What number/level could you cope with?'

■ 'What could you do that would reduce it?'

As the numbers come down, most young people recognise that they can cope. They relax and the pain subsides. (See page 57.)

■ Moral judgments

Would you allow your child to experiment with performance-enhancing drugs in order to win? Issues that sport faces today will be in the public domain tomorrow.

There may come a time when genetic scientists say, 'For £25,000, you can have a child with competitive aggression and huge muscle power. That child could make you a fortune.' Would you be tempted?

Safeguarding the long-term health and safety of our children is of paramount importance. It is vital to ensure that we take well-informed decisions, and that we involve our young people in issues relating to their future, rather than leading with our own ambition.

Clouded judgments

How often do we take stock of the long-term consequences of our statements or actions?

A few children as young as six years old are currently being signed to football exclusivity contracts, yet very few young protégées make it to premier level. What happens to their talent for any other sport or physical activity, if they have not been able to develop fundamental skills when their bodies were most capable of learning and adapting?

It is valuable to look carefully at the pros and cons of each choice we make for our children.

■ Give me some space!

Losing our self-control doesn't help!

Children do need boundaries. Often a calm, clear, quiet and firm 'no' or 'later' is more effective than matching levels of volume and hostility, because the young person may not be in a fit state to hear clearly or debate rationally.

We also need to check levels of stress, tiredness, frustration, excess sugar in the diet, over-heatedness and so on, in our young people and ourselves. Taking these factors into account will allow us to make wiser decisions.

With stress levels high and time pressing, many of us feel emotionally challenged when additional demands come from our young people.

Giving young people time, while encouraging them to understand that we need our private time too, is necessary and healthy for both parties.

Guidance for parents and grandparents on asking questions

I am so grateful to have been introduced to the power of questioning while my children – Adrian and Pete – were still only five and three years old. I have much enjoyed the quality of our friendship and, by encouraging our sons to generate their choices while they were still very young, my wife and I have not experienced our boys fighting us for their independence as they grew up. One challenge for us was trusting them and letting go.

■ Try asking!

There was some early learning for me. Not long after I started running courses, teaching others how to become more effective questioners, I was experiencing a little frustration as my younger son, Pete, was coming in from playschool and dropping his coat on the floor. After many days of telling him to pick up his coat, I heard myself thinking, 'How many times must I tell him this!?' Immediately it hit me that I was *telling*, not *asking*, and therefore not engaging his brain. So, the next day, as soon as he dropped his coat, I pointed at his coat and asked, 'Pete, where else could you put that?' For the first time, I saw him engage his brain and, after a few seconds, he suggested his room. He dashed upstairs and probably dropped it there! The next day, the same thing happened and again I asked him, 'Pete, where else could you put your coat?' This time, he suggested the cupboard, very near the front door. That was the last time I had to say anything! My question had raised his awareness of what he was doing and he took responsibility for hanging up his coat. Problem solved.

■ The practical use of a scale

When Adrian, my elder son, was still only five years old, I asked for his help. I let him know that I was concerned when he screamed, and that I wanted him to give me a pain rating on a 1–10 scale. Ten meant I would need to call an ambulance, and 1 meant that it hurt very little. (If a young person is not happy with numbers, he or she can find a scale in words.) Within days, it worked brilliantly. I heard an almighty scream from the back garden and I ran. Adrian had his hand on the back of his head and there were serious tears of pain. I asked what happened and he replied, 'I bumped my head!' I said I was really sorry and asked if he could give it a pain rating. He paused and said, 'It's an 8!' I had a look and felt the bump rising on the back of his head with the speed you see on cartoons, so I asked him if he would like to come in or put some witch hazel on it, to help to take the bruise out.

'No, thanks!'

'Would you like to sit down?'

'No, thanks!'

'What number is it on now?'

'Umm, 7.'

I asked him how it had happened and he explained that he had been climbing over the five-bar gate when his foot had slipped and he had fallen backwards and hit his head on something really hard. Again, I said I was sorry and asked if there was anything he would like me to do. He said, 'No' and I asked him again what number it was now?

'Oh, 5. Forget it, Dad!'

He seemed considerably recovered from the shock; he was aware that his pain level was reducing and he took responsibility to cope with his current level of discomfort. As he charged off, I called, 'Do come back inside if you feel like it.'

I heard him yell, 'Okay' as he disappeared from view and that was the last I saw of him that afternoon.

The questions had generated his self-awareness, and meant that he took personal responsibility for assessing his state and that he chose to cope with it.

We do not want to deny our young people their experience. It is real for them at the time. So if someone starts whingeing or complaining to us, we can ask, 'How much is this bothering you – on a 1-10 scale?' The same whinge can come from a minor irritation that they just want to share in order to let it go, or from something that is troubling them deeply and that they need to clarify and choose to do something about.

■ Why is awareness so important?

You cannot consciously change something that you are unaware of. Every positive change starts with increased awareness and the choice to do something that will lead towards a positive resolution.

■ Converting statements into questions

Often words will race into our thoughts as statements or advice. However, if we want to be 'Guardians of the Flame' (see Preface), can we restrain ourselves from giving that instant advice and take ten seconds to convert our suggestion into an awareness-raising question? For example: 'Hurry up and get dressed' might be changed to 'What's the shortest time it could take you to get dressed?'; or 'Don't touch that!' to 'What's the reason I don't want you to touch that?'

It is my belief that any question that makes the young person think is coaching or mentoring them. For me the words 'coaching' and 'counselling' have huge similarity. In each case, we can start on the young person's agenda by asking for their aims and hopes, and their perception of current reality. In all cases it may be appropriate to give advice. However, ultimately we are aiming to have the young person take responsibility for their choices. In counselling the choice is often made in response to a problem. In coaching situations that may be true as well, although the choice is usually made more proactively.

■ Bedtime

As a parent or grandparent, our instant reaction when we find our young person watching television at an hour well beyond their bedtime might be to feel angry and tell them to go to bed immediately. However, we might self-monitor our instant feeling of wanting to yell at them, and instead take a deep breath and ask, 'How aware are you of the time?'

I tried this with Pete, when he was about 11 or 12. I asked how much longer he was planning on watching television. He told me that the programme ended at 10.30pm. I then asked him how much homework he had to do for the next day, to which he replied, 'Only half an hour.'

I asked when he planned to do it and he said, 'In the morning.'

When I next passed the room and it was after 10.30 and he was still there, I simply said, 'It's after 10.30 and it's your choice, but we are off to bed. Good night.'

I have no idea what time he went to bed, but a couple of days later, at about 8.30, Pete said, 'Do you mind if I go to bed?' I replied, 'Of course not, Pete. It's your life. Have a good sleep. We'll see you in the morning.'

From then on he set his alarm to get his homework done each morning. I saw our parental role as supporters of our children's interests and endeavours, to provide as much opportunity as we could, but mainly to help them to become self-responsible adults. If our constant intent is to generate greater awareness and responsibility in them, they will become less dependent on us and other people for every piece of new learning and behaviour.

■ 'Yes, but' versus 'Yes, and'

How often have we heard people say, 'Yes, but...'? Everything before the 'but' is being effectively negated. Receiving a 'Yes, but...' response often frustrates, deflates or angers the listener.

It sets up confrontation. If we can answer with 'Yes, *and…*', it is more likely that our young people will feel acknowledged for what they have contributed and feel that we are adding something to their thinking.

If we disagree seriously with some of what has been said, how can we best convey that without dismissing everything? It may take us time, and yet doing it will validate the speaker, who will be more willing to listen to our subsequent ideas. We could start with specifics:

'I like your idea of this, and I strongly disagree with that part, for this reason… What do you think of this as an alternative to that?'

Our intent should be to keep their flame of enthusiasm alive and burning while still making our contribution.

■ Generating self-reflection

Have we underestimated the capacity of the young to choose to change? During a follow-on day from a business-mentoring course, one businessman who had used questioning with his six-year-old daughter told me a story. He said that she was a bit of a drama queen. She also loved the Harry Potter books, in which out-of-body experiences are not impossible. When she was in a bit of a state, he asked his daughter if she would be willing to act like Harry and put herself into her Dad's position and tell him what she saw.

She paused and then said, 'An angry girl!'

He then asked her, 'Would you want to play with her?'

She gave a sharp, hard, 'Yes!'

He said, 'Look a bit closer. Would you really?'

His daughter's voice softened and she said, 'Well, maybe not.'

In seconds he had questioned this little person into a degree of self-recognition that could have a powerful effect on her future behaviour. With increased self-awareness she will be able to choose who and how she wants to be.

Self-reflection and judgment were called for when my children were young. If they had been caught doing something mean or unacceptable, I would ask, 'What punishment do you think you deserve for doing that?' or, What do you think the consequences should be for doing that?'

I was quite amazed that they both, individually, gave themselves harder punishment than I would have given out. They would reply with things like, 'I think I should stay in my room for an hour' or 'I think I shouldn't have any pocket money next week.' We would then have a brief discussion as to what was reasonable and fair.

A few months after another business course one young mum told me of her experience coaching her little boy.

It was a cold day and she told him he should put on his coat. He said that he didn't want to, but she insisted and put it on him. A moment or two later she found that his coat was on the floor behind him!

She told me that she said calmly that it was cold outside and that when he went out to play in the break time he might be very cold if he didn't have his coat, but it was his choice. She busied herself with something else and then heard a small voice behind her. She turned to see him with his coat on, saying that he'd decided that he would wear his coat today. What a truly empowering time this lady had generated for her child. He aligned with his mum's logic, but by his choice rather than imposition.

■ Projecting fear

One challenge to parents is to avoid projecting personal fears on to our young people. I witnessed a little girl of five running down a ramp from a multi-storey shopping complex. The ramp led to the pavement and then the road. The child was screaming with delight and the mother was yelling for her to stop. She did stop, but only as she reached the edge of the pavement.

In her fear the mother ran up and hit the child hard on her bottom, which made the child cry. She was yelling, 'You're never to do that again! Do you hear me?'

What message the child received, I'm not sure. Did she mean 'Never run again'? Had the child even heard the mother yelling for her to stop? There was no explanation from the mother as to why she was upset nor any explanation of the consequences of running towards a road full of moving traffic. The mother's action was an expression of her true concern for the life of her child; however, that message was surely lost on the child.

Are we willing to take the time to explain to our young people what has upset us and ask them to reflect on the consequences of their actions?

I remember my wife finding Pete, when he was five or six years old, climbing in the rafters of the barn near our house, probably four or more metres from the floor. Inside her there were knots of considerable concern, but she managed to prevent her nerves being projected on to him, as she calmly asked if he could show her how he could get down from there. He said, 'Okay, it's easy!' and proceeded to climb down with nimble ease. The end product was a win for both parties.

■ Abuse of power

This book is dedicated to listening attentively and asking effective questions. Smacking a child contradicts these principles directly.

It is odd that, if an adult strikes any other adult, they are laying themselves open to being sued. Yet many parents are still keen to retain the right to strike those most vulnerable in their care. Some back their claims with such statements as 'Spare the rod and spoil the child' or 'A short sharp smack is quick and justified' or 'It never did me any harm!'

What would we feel like now if someone gave us a smack? We could feel angry and ready to retaliate or perhaps we might feel humiliated. Why should we think that the reaction of our young people would be any different? And what is it doing to our child's self-esteem? For me, striking a child is the ultimate abuse of adult power, and it is modelling the use of violence.

Where can the child go for safety? Are they not totally dependent on us for food, accommodation and protection? As adults, we hold all the power and control.

We are usually bigger, stronger, have say over whether they stay or go, have or have not. For many years after birth, young people are truly dependent on us. We have a responsibility to nurture them and care for and about them. It is now a part of the United Nations' declaration of human rights that adults are not to hit children.

Being a parent is a complicated, exhausting and incredibly important job. We may not always remember our greater intentions when trying to protect or encourage our children, and we will all make mistakes. But if we get into the habit of asking questions, rather than imposing our solutions and ideas, we will find that job easier and more rewarding.

3

The role of the teacher

Most teachers should take huge credit for their dedication and their intent to help in the education and development of our young people. This has been extremely challenging, with numerous government interventions generating an overload in paper work. Also, because of the prescriptive nature of the curriculum, some feel straitjacketed in their ability to be creative and responsive. This last factor has contributed to 'turning off' large numbers of pupils, who have become more disruptive as a result, which has added to the pressure on teachers to act more like police. This can lead to further student alienation and can become a vicious cycle.

I heard one teacher say that, in a noisy classroom, he remained calm and repeated 'Sit down' until eventually the young people were numbed into submission! Are we then surprised if these young people are bored or angered that they 'must do what they are told', and cannot wait to be freed from the requirement of attending school? Some students feel as though it is a prison sentence! Is it any wonder?

Creating monsters

■ Providing role-models

What is this adult thinking?

What is the likely effect on George? Humiliation? Embarrassment? Consternation? Loss of self-esteem and confidence?

And what are the others supposed to learn?

Negative learning experiences are counter-productive. We should strive to provide *positive* role-models for our children.

Labelling

Much as we may wish to label a young person 'thick' or 'stupid', our assistance is needed at times of crisis or major learning.

It is important to assess what state the young person is in and to ask:

- ◼ 'What happened?'

- ◼ 'What do you need to learn, so as not to repeat the mistake?'

Few young people *intend* to cause catastrophe!

The learning partnership

■ Get involved!

Recent surveys show that 60 per cent of children are bored with school and do not want to be there. If we are primarily following our own agenda, how can we expect young people to be interested?

This is made more difficult when teachers are asked to follow set curricula from government guidelines. This can be mind-numbing and constraining for some teachers as well as for the young people. How do we engage their hearts and minds?

When there is no choice, the answer may be as simple as asking them *how* they would like to investigate a subject. How much can we ask our students for their choice of course content? And do educators need to challenge overly restrictive curricula?

■ Can we raise their self-awareness first?

Most people value feedback from a more experienced person.
However, to help the young person to grow, we might first ask
for their experience if we intend to develop their self-awareness.

When we do give feedback, it needs to be specific, such as,
'When you rush the last stanza, my experience is that some of
the melody is lost.'

PETE, LET ME SHOW YOU HOW TO DRAW THAT
PLEASE DON'T DRAW ON MY PICTURE
I HAVE TO
CAN'T YOU JUST TELL ME?
PETE YOU'VE GOT AN ATTITUDE PROBLEM

■ 'I'm the teacher!' – stifling creativity?

Who has the attitude problem?

When young people are attempting to develop their creativity, how damaging is it for us to impose our way? Can we not allow them to experiment within safe limits?

We may believe we know best, and yet we need to be wise enough to go with their enthusiasm, and find out what they would like or need from us.

■ Discussing the options

As young people become more self-aware, many become quite self-conscious. They may feel peer-group pressure to conform, to look and sound a certain way or to avoid standing out.

Before investing time and effort, ask the child how interested and willing they are to be involved in what you are doing.

Moving forward

■ Keep it simple!

Do we sometimes try to convey too much or do we over-complicate things?

How can we keep things simple?

■ Asking before judging

If we have an issue with someone's poor performance, one valuable approach is to express our concern, then ask for his or her view.

Before we raise this, it will be necessary to gather evidence. For example, if we have a concern in sport that the person is not passing the ball as much as others and that this is affecting the team's morale and performance, we may need to keep track of just how many passes are made in comparison with others; how many times the ball is lost through trying to pass too late, and so on. We might also ask the person what alternatives they may have and if they would be willing to try a different approach.

The bottom line will always be to encourage the person to become more aware and take responsibility to be more helpful or constructive.

Guidance for teachers on asking questions

■ Working together

In the early 1970s, Professor Chris Argyris from Harvard told us – his students – that: 'People should be involved in decisions that affect them personally'. They can feel valued and are more likely to contribute their energy. There is a great deal of evidence that involving people will help bring out the best in them.

When I was teaching at Millfield School, the founding Headmaster, Jack Meyer, told me that in his experience, if someone had a talent or an interest in an activity that they were allowed to spend some lesson time on during the regular school day, their interest in everything else lifted as well. That meant it was better for tennis or piano practice to be included during academic lesson times, so it became a part of the young person's daily routine and improved their all-round success.

Self-determination is a real asset to feeling empowered. A.S. Neil, in his experimental school, Summerhill, set tremendous store by this approach. The children had full responsibility for setting and implementing their own school and living rules and for the consequences of breaking them. Students took very seriously the requirement to assume responsibility for themselves and each other, and they grew significantly through that involvement.

No matter how inspiring a teacher's words may be, the student's memory of what was taught will fade. Only if his or her words motivate a young person will their enthusiasm grow. So how do we use questions to generate motivation? We simply have to prompt thought in our young people by asking them to reflect on what it is that motivates and interests them.

■ Going at their own pace

At St John's School in Marlborough, Wiltshire, the Head
Teacher, Patrick Hazelwood, decided to embark on an
experiment. A number of young people, aged around 11 years
old, were asked to choose in which area(s) they would like to
learn beyond the national curriculum. In the trial year,
2001–2002, several of these young students advanced their level
in their chosen subjects by several years – some by as many as
five years. Some thrived and others were a bit daunted by being
asked to be so self-responsible. They certainly were not used to
it and some were probably not ready for it. But what do the
many positive results tell us about self-motivation? They show
that human beings have a real desire to learn and that, given an
opportunity, many will take it and thrive. By 2005 Patrick was
addressing the idea that traditional homework should be
relegated to the dustbin. Not that work at home should be
neglected, but that it should be creative, project- and theme-
based rather than limited by insistence on textbook prescriptive
'right answers'. The idea is that school should be advancing
personal development and generating interest in life-long
learning.

How often have we taken the easy way, encouraging young
people to learn what we want them to know, when we want
them to know it, in the sequence that we believe is best for
them? By taking all the responsibility on ourselves, they are let
off the hook. It was not their idea anyway! Why should they
care or bother? I am not suggesting that we abdicate
responsibility or that we abandon our children. Our gift is to
engage and involve them in their plans and hopes. It does not
mean we should not have input; the key is when and how.
Primarily, we should act as a catalyst and resource, rather than
doing all the thinking for them. Our challenge is to trust that
allowing young people to make their own choices, advance their
ambitions and go with their enthusiasm, will make them and
us, feel much more fulfilled.

■ What do 'the best' do? Collaborative learning

Hungarian schools have the best maths results in Europe.
A BBC2 documentary showed an example of a maths class in
Hungary. The teacher was seen explaining a new concept to the
class of 11-year-olds. He then asked who had clearly
understood and, from the two or three, he asked for a student
volunteer to share at the front of the class what they had
grasped. After the student explained what he had learned, the
teacher asked who else now understood. With perhaps a third of
them having their hand raised, he then asked each of the
students who raised their hands to explain to small groups
around them what they had understood. He then had the time
to circulate and assist as needed. He facilitated further learning
through effectively questioning the young people on their
understanding and applications. This highly involving process
was giving many young people the chance to explain new
material to a peer. As most people know, we really learn what we
have to explain to others. The young people who are willing to
do this inevitably advance, and take their own learning to a
higher level. Their peers may see the subject matter from a
slightly different angle, as the words that the recent learner uses
may make the concept more accessible and more easily
understood. The process also helps to make learning an
inclusive process.

■ Judging and feedback

Quite often, young people will expect our feedback. 'How was
that?' they will ask, as they defer to our judgment. When I
started teaching 'A' level Economics students at Millfield
School, I remember asking which student would be willing to
read their paper to the class. I asked the other students to listen
and afterwards say what they thought was good about it, then
what they felt could have been included or expressed differently
in a way that would have enhanced it, and then to give it a

grade. At first they were a little uncomfortable, but that soon passed and they become supportive and made sensible, constructive suggestions. Interestingly, within a small margin, they agreed on what they would give each paper on a 1–10 scale. During the first lesson, after the last paper had been read, they asked me what the 'right' grades were. I shared with them that mine was also 'an opinion', that I was only slightly more experienced than they were and that I believed that their judgment was very close to, if not exactly the same as mine. If I had known then what I know now, I would have started with the student who had presented their paper and asked them to assess the merit of their own paper, then to say what they would do differently to make it any better if they had the chance to do it again. Then I would have asked for their fellow students' views, and would have followed those with my own.

If we are asked to give feedback, it needs to be detailed and specific, rather than judgmental. For example, 'That was clear and passionate. In my view it would have had had increased impact if you had added more illustrations to justify your enthusiasm for the issue.'

The timing of feedback is also important. We need to ask ourselves whether the young person is in the necessary emotional and intellectual state to take on board our positive intent. Bearing in mind that children mature at different rates we may need to adjust our style to match their capability and maturity.

■ Honesty

During my teacher-training term, with a group of bright 'A' level Economics students, I was asked a question that I could not answer. I simply acknowledged that it was a great question and that I would find an answer by the next day, but that I also expected the student to see what he could find out, too. Did I lose credibility in the eyes of the students? Possibly, but I would have lost much more if I had tried and failed to disguise my ignorance. I was also showing that the teacher may not be the fount of all information and that the student has a responsibility, too. The encyclopaedic computer information bank *Encarta* contains more knowledge than any one teacher can possibly retain and recall, even if they are awesomely well read. I welcome young people thinking and challenging the subjects under discussion. They stand on our shoulders and we can facilitate their climb.

In the face of so many young people not wanting to learn what we are required to teach, we may feel massive frustration. Adding to that the burden of writing constant evaluations of the progress of these unwilling souls may generate a sense of overwhelming and gloom. However, the teacher's role is critical for their students' future. Can we retain the vision of what brought many of us into teaching? What can we do that will help to inspire the hopes and positive intent for the future of our young people? How can we best sustain their and our enthusiasm? Perhaps we should start by asking them.

4

The role of the coach

Coach knows best?

We are fortunate in sport, because most of the young people who come to us are interested and willing to take part. It is true that, in most people, the desire to improve is innate. One question is how we can help young people in their quest to get the best out of themselves. Another question is how to balance instruction and questioning; this applies to learning in everyday life, too.

■ Let me tell you how it's gonna be...

For some people 'coaching' means 'instruction'.

Our gift to young people is to help them to learn how to self-coach or at least to self-discover, as well as learning from our input. Once they become involved, they can contribute much to their own development.

The GROW model of questioning is often used to enable those we are coaching to focus on and clarify their core issues:

Goal – What do you really want to achieve?

Reality – What is happening at the moment?

Options – What could you do?

Will – What will you do?

Most issues can be moved forward positively by asking these types of questions. (See also page 145.)

WHY WON'T YOU PASS THE BALL THE WAY I'VE JUST SHOWN YOU?
BUT SIR, THAT WAY DOESN'T FEEL RIGHT FOR ME
DO IT MY WAY OR YOU WON'T PLAY FOR MY TEAM!

■ 'My way or the highway!'

Can we help young performers to find their best way?

Many of us believe that we must change young people to fit our ideal model of the right way to do something – whether it be sport or any other human endeavour.

Which came first, good performers or instruction books and instructors? Obviously, the good performers came first; then we try to implement their good practice. Beginning with good practice may be fine. However, without experimenting with the young person's way, we may never find the next Borg double-handed tennis backhand or the Fosbury flop high jump or the Picasso painting, and we certainly will not find our performer's best way.

I can hear some saying, 'But I do not have time for individual experimentation.' Do we not? Even with a large group, we can ask each person to pay attention to the least comfortable aspect of their play and to experiment with how they would *like* it to feel. This has the benefit of self-discovery and the effect is that the performer will develop to a higher level.

The key is to find an appropriate balance of self-discovery and external input.

■ 'They did it MY way!'

How many of us are stuck in our ways, still adhering rigidly to doing things the way we were taught originally?

How easy or difficult is it for us to recognise that there is often more than one right answer or one right way to do things?

What assumptions are we making about what interests our young people and what they want from us?

What *do* they want from us?

We could find out by asking simple questions:

■ 'What interests you?'

■ 'What do you want to know from me?'

And if they are unsure:

■ 'Would you like a suggestion?' or

■ 'Would you want me to tell you what I'm noticing?'

Asking the performer whether they would like a suggestion may sound rather odd, but the rationale is that the young person will have been using the creative right-side of their brain to discover their own best way of movement. Our questions shift their focus into left-brain analysis, encouraging them to ask themselves: 'Does this make sense for me?'

Most important, after we have shared our thoughts, ask the young person what *they* think or how they might use the ideas.

Motivation

■ Challenging or bullying?

An alternative approach to the one above, whether in sport, academia or in any other activity, could be:

■ 'Do you think/feel you did yourself justice?'

And, in the case of this cartoon, after some recovery time:

■ 'What level of effort did you put in that time?' (Awareness generating.)

■ 'What would enable you to increase it next time?' (Responsibility generating.)

■ Achievement costs, and here's where you start paying...

Sometimes it can be useful to act as the conscience for young performers. This is especially true when getting them started, by encouraging them with: 'Just take the first step!'

However, before giving a supportive push, we need to hear the young person's agreement that this would help them. We also need to ensure that we are not harming their health and that we are not killing their enthusiasm. We could ask:

■ Would you like me to hold you to completing this?'

■ Curb your enthusiasm!

When has our enthusiasm for an activity clouded our judgment?

When have our aspirations for young people led us to push them when they did not want to be pushed?

We may think we know what is best for the young person – but is our ambition for their esteem or for ours?

Whose agenda are we on?

It may help our perspective if we consider what it would be like to be the young person in this situation. What feelings and thoughts might they be experiencing?

■ What do WE need to do?

If we start by focusing on the young person's agenda, they will be much more willing to hear and engage with our agenda.

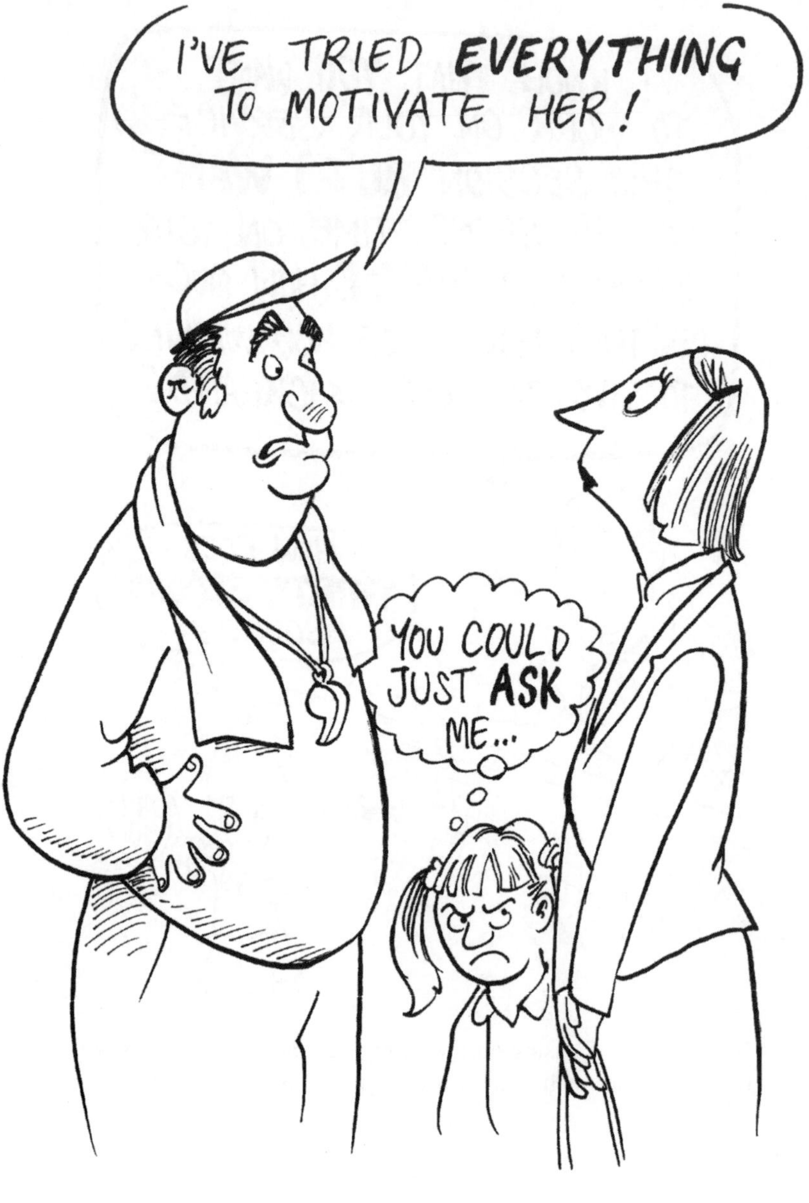
I'VE TRIED EVERYTHING TO MOTIVATE HER!
YOU COULD JUST ASK ME...

■ Try asking ME!

How often have we tried to be nice? We may have offered opportunities and all sorts of suggestions, without realising that we may be taking away the young person's ownership of their activities.

The simple solution is to ask:

■ 'What interests you?' or

■ 'What would motivate you?'

Getting emotional

■ Under stress?

I HAVEN'T GOT ALL DAY – GET IN THE POOL!

Our 'emotional intelligence' can be assessed by how well we recognise the effect or impact that we have on others and by how well we manage our own emotions and responses, particularly when we are under stress.

One of our challenges is to find a way for our young people to become more self-responsible and aware of the impact and effects of their actions and inaction on other people.

Sample questions:

■ 'What effect do you think it has on me, when you act like this?'

■ 'What could you be doing that would help to move things forward?'

■ 'What are you willing to do differently to help this situation?'

■ Taking charge of emotions

Part of our uniqueness as humans is our free will.

How well do we challenge our young people to prioritise their time and energy, to make choices and to recognise the consequences of their actions?

Sometimes, we could simply ask them:

■ 'What are your options, and what are the pros and cons of each?'

■ Getting lost in your own feelings

Encouragement, enthusiasm and presenting challenges can all be positive and necessary attributes of a coach.

Our love for an activity may deny our young people the opportunity for their own free will. How can we avoid this?

Sometimes, they may ask for a push because they really need that support.

However, we also need to ask our performers what they want or need from us; and ideally be able to recognise the feelings that they are experiencing.

■ Losing the spirit of the sport

We have all come across intransigent officials. Most probably
have good intentions but seem not to appreciate the damage
they inflict on the enthusiasm of the young person and their
parents or coaches. If we are in the official position, can we look
from the other person's viewpoint as well as our own?

If we find ourselves bound by rulebooks, perhaps we need to
look at our intent. What is the main purpose of the event? If it
is to provide opportunity for competition in good spirit, then
will our 'letter of the law' approach kill the spirit? What would
be a healthy compromise that satisfies all parties?

Perhaps we need to look at our own needs and drives. If we were the official in the situation illustrated, would we exert appropriate levels of power and control?

Do we hide behind rules because we do not want to be bothered – either to think through a reasonable argument or because we do not want the hassle of taking action?

Feeding back

■ One at a time!

It is important to focus on only one thing at a time.

At any one moment in time *single appropriate focus* produces the best performance because even two foci can reduce effective performance by at least 10 per cent.

Can we encourage our young people to prioritise by choosing one point of focus, at any moment?

Sample questions:

■ '*Where* are you paying attention?'

■ 'When this happens, where is your focus?'

■ 'Where or what would be the best place to have your attention?'

■ Staying focused

Once we have agreed on one point of focus, how fair is it to criticise the young person on a different point that we have not asked them to concentrate on?

Immediate feedback needs to be on the requested focus.

For example: 'That was great action with the left arm. Let's focus next time on the right knee.'

■ Timing!

Timing is everything!

When have you received a useful comment or question which was expressed too soon or too late to have a positive effect?

We need to ask ourselves:

■ When will be the most appropriate time for this question/comment, to have the most constructive effect?

■ You tell me!

Some young people equate answering questions with the need to get the 'right' answer. This is unhelpful as it can stop them from contributing simply and honestly by taking stock of their own experience.

If they are desperate for us to lead them, we are being young-person-centred by giving them some guidelines or our feedback. However, we need to explain to them our intent, to ensure they are actively involved in their own performance.

Inputs from both young people and us should help them to reach higher levels of performance.

Guidance for coaches on asking questions

■ Coaching young people

Matching the young person's expectations

The cartoon on page 107 comes from an experience I had when visiting my university coach in Boston, shortly after I was introduced to coaching by questioning. He was also the coach for the Scituate High School girls' team. One of his students was in her last year and heading for medical school. He said that she was a pretty good hurdler but he would like me to have a training session with her. I thought, 'Oh great, an opportunity to try out my questioning skills!' I told her that I would like to ask her some questions after she ran over a few hurdles. When she came back I said, 'What did you notice?' She looked like a rabbit caught in car headlights and answered, 'Nothing!' So I explained that she might notice something like a twist of her upper body as she landed or that she might feel some stopping of forward momentum as her leg touched the ground after the hurdle, and I sent her off for another run. I asked the same question on her return. 'What did you notice that time?' She again replied, 'Nothing!' and although I could see that she felt agitated and uncomfortable, I was naïve enough to try again. When I had the same response again, I gave up and asked her if she'd like me to tell her what I had noticed. At this point I saw her visibly relax and she said, 'Yes, please.'

Here was a bright student who was used to getting the answers right, and in this case did not know what the 'right' answer was. I had not explained that there was no 'right' answer, or that I was looking for her to develop from her own experience as well as my input.

Obviously she was not used to being asked to input from her experience. In addition, I was working so much according to my own agenda that I did not initially respond well to her current need – to be told. If I had been a bit more experienced I would have explained the intent of my questions, letting her know that she could learn just as much, if not more, from what she was experiencing, as from what I was seeing. I would have asked her to let me know when she felt comfortable giving me some feedback, that I would still be happy to tell her what I saw, but that I would eventually like her to speak first. This would have encouraged her independence and enhanced her inner authority. It would also have meant that she could learn from her experiences when I wasn't there. The ideal was that both she and I would be involved in her learning and, that way, higher levels could be reached than either one of us could attain exclusively.

Asking for self-awareness and self-responsibility

Many young people initially feel awkward at being asked to be more self-responsible. When I was coaching at Boston University, one of the students strained the ligament in the arch of her left foot. She asked me to tell her when to start jogging again. I said that she had to listen to her own body. She would have to monitor its progress and decide when the time was right for her. I said that I could not tell her, as I could not feel how the injury was recovering. She was quite upset at my perceived non-cooperation. In her view, I probably knew what was best and was refusing to give her a definitive time when she should start to run again. However, several weeks later she came back and told me that although she had not really liked my advice – to be self-responsible – she had learned so much about herself by paying attention to her body's feedback that she wanted me to know how valuable it had been. Sometimes a Guardian may have to be cruel to be kind.

Mike Sprechlen was coach to Sir Steve Redgrave, when Steve was rowing for his first 'pairs' gold medal with Mike Holmes. Mike came on a coaching-by-questioning course that I was running. During the course he told me that, technically, he had taught Redgrave and Holmes all that he knew, and was feeling that he had little more he could contribute. He recognised that they were feeling things that he could not even see on video, so the questioning technique was a huge gift to him. He said that this would enable him to ask them questions that would involve their senses, for example: 'Using a 1–10 scale, how much are you two in synchronised timing, on the catch?' And by increasing their awareness of their process, their performance could be enhanced.

■ Working with Olympic medallists – the positive impact of awareness and choice

Mark Rowland

I have had the privilege of working with several Olympic medallists. Before the 1988 Olympics, Mark Rowland came to me to have a session on hurdling. He was intending to change events and try to qualify for the 3000m steeplechase for the upcoming Olympics. He was a very good miler, but was not going to make an impact like Coe or Ovett, who were both world record holders and Olympic medallists in the 800m and 1500m. Mark had good strength and ran well in cross-country races. After a session at the track, where I helped him to practise some key hurdling movements, we sat down to discuss his chances in the Games. He said that he was unhappy with the quality of his hurdling. I asked Mark how well he thought the Africans hurdled. He said that they were certainly not brilliant, and he had to admit that they won in spite of that. I asked how his speed compared with their speed over a mile. He acknowledged that he was faster. I then asked how his strength compared in distance-running terms. He again had to admit that he had good endurance strength. So I asked him for how long he thought he could stay with the Kenyans during the Games. He made that a goal and his performance was a revelation. He broke the British record by seven seconds and won a bronze medal in the 1988 Olympics. He was overjoyed.

Obviously, much else would have gone on in Mark's preparation, with other coaches, and a mass of hard work. However, my questions were aimed at helping him to take a reality check. They moved his thinking and focus from self-criticism, for not having a skill in one area and very little time to practise that skill before the Olympics, to looking at the strengths that could compensate and might outweigh any potential weakness. All credit to Mark for transferring to a new event and holding his head, and heart, together to achieve an exceptional performance. He has since become an outstanding coach, successfully using an involving style himself.

Debbie Flintoff-King

Not long before those same Olympics, Debbie Flintoff-King, a 400m hurdler from Australia, came to stay with us. While we drove to my home, I asked questions of Debbie, concerning her goals for the Games. She said that she was aiming to make the final. 'And then?' I asked. She had not thought much further than that. I asked where she thought she could finish. She explained that although she was usually a couple of metres ahead at the halfway stage, she was usually caught by the end of the second bend and, in the home straight, the German and Russian contestants would come past her. I asked another reality question: what prompted her to be going out so hard? She explained that, in order to make her stride pattern effective, using 15 strides between each hurdle, she had to run fast. I asked whether she might hold a stronger pace around the second bend if she ran the first half of her race slightly slower. She said, 'Yes, but I don't think I can hold the length of stride at a slower pace.' I asked if she would be willing to experiment with that. She agreed and, in the next track hurdling session, discovered that she could run slightly slower and still maintain her stride length in the first 200m. It would make the difference of only a couple of tenths of a second, but that can be enough to retain sufficient energy. I then asked, 'If you did that, do you think you would have the strength to decelerate by only one or two tenths of a second between each second-bend hurdle?' She gave me a strong-voiced: 'Yes, definitely.'

When we reached home, I took a piece of paper and wrote down the times of a slightly slower first 200 metres, a second bend with a less dramatic slowing than usual, and then the same run in time. It worked out that she could break the world record, and therefore could think about running to win! She looked for hours at that piece of paper and its additions of time. She took it up to bed and brought it back down with her to breakfast the next morning. Obviously, many factors make an Olympic champion, not least the hours of intense training. However, I do know that some of her thinking on those questions positively affected Debbie's belief that it was possible to win. It changed her perception of her chances and then her intent. She judged her race astonishingly well. She caught the Russian Tatyana Ledovskaya on the finish line, winning the Olympic gold by one hundredth of a second.

A fraction of a second can be all the difference in having or avoiding a serious accident. It can be all it takes to notice an expression of pain or panic. It could be the time we take to change our mind and make a poor or great decision. As Guardians, we have an opportunity to generate changes in thinking or attitudes that can make a big difference to an outcome. Our questions can have a major effect on what our young people are doing with their thoughts. If we can help to increase their level of self and situational awareness, they will have a better chance of coping well with their upcoming challenges. With Debbie, I was challenging her assumptions. My questions helped her to redirect her focus and energy distribution.

Sally Gunnell

Four years later, prior to the 1992 Olympics, I was asked to work with Sally Gunnell, another 400m hurdler. She had been a British Champion in the sprint hurdles and, just as I had done, moved to the longer-distance hurdles race. She had had some trouble committing herself to holding her stride length at the end of a championship race and the stutter steps had cost her several metres and a win. I found out that she had not been introduced to visualisation, in which the mind is used to rehearse situations. Sally took to the idea quickly and effectively. I used questioning to help her to visualise exactly how she would execute her races and, in particular, to go for the last hurdle as if it were the first in a sprint hurdle race. She had a great capacity to do this and changed her mental attitude to one of positive commitment towards achieving the stride pattern that she wanted. She sailed through the Olympic trials and held her composure through each qualifying round at the Games. In the Olympic final she came past the American Sandra Farmer Patrick in the last 40 metres of her race. Afterwards, she explained to the press how she knew that she could do that because she had rehearsed it so many times in her imagination. The following year she asked me what she could have as a target, as she was number one in the world. I asked her what other goals she might have. She said she would like to break the world record. I asked her when her ideal time would be to do that. Her response was, 'In the final of the World Championships.' Each aspect was questioned and a strategy produced. Sally won the 1993 World Championships in a new world record.

Much credit goes to Bruce Longden, her coach. He helped her get her body into brilliant condition. How many people do you know who have the technical ability and conditioning to perform well but do not execute well under pressure? That implies that their focus or their attitude could be an issue. My gift was to help Sally to harness her mental capacity to bring the best out of herself when she most wanted to.

■ A supportive push – with the performer's agreement

Taking the first step

Sometimes a supportive push can be really helpful *but* there has to be an agreement that it is what the young person wants and that it is in their best long-term interests. I remember vividly the help given to me by Billy Smith, my Irish-American coach at Boston University, during a memorable session in my build-up to the 1968 Olympic gold. My recall is clear because I found the session so difficult. He acted as my conscience. Prior to the session, Billy and I had agreed that the ideal workout would be six times 400 metres, run at a good pace, with 10 minutes' recovery between each repetition. I managed three of the set before I felt shattered. When run hard, the 400m had a knack of producing this feeling! But I said to myself, 'If you dig deep and really concentrate, you can get out one more at this pace.' With a strong degree of will power I hung on and hung on and crossed the line in the required time. Enough was enough. I went and lay down behind the seating around the track. In no time at all, Billy sent a student round to let me know my 10 minutes were up. I went to Billy and explained that my legs were gone. He put his hands on his legs and said, 'I can't feel a thing. Just take the first step.' I told him that I could not do another repetition, but he would not take no for an answer, and repeated more firmly, 'Just take the first step!' I tried several more excuses as to why I could not do any more and it became apparent that I was not going to get away with doing nothing. I heard again, 'Just take the first step!'

Although my legs felt like lead, I started running and, to my amazement, I discovered that I could actually get around the track at close to the same pace again. It was at some cost. I crossed the line, staggered to the outside of the track and was physically sick. My head was pounding and ached badly but I made it 10 metres further to outside the seating area and collapsed, flat on my back on the ground. Ten minutes later the same student was standing over me, saying that the coach was waiting. I said, 'He's got to be joking! I have a splitting headache. I lost my lunch and my legs are like jelly!' He said, 'You'd better tell him.' With great effort, I rolled over and forced myself on to my hands and knees, then pulled myself up to standing and, with a throbbing head and raw throat, tottered over to the coach, who pointed out that I was already late starting. I told him what I felt like and that I had nothing left. His comment: 'But we agreed to six!' I knew that we had agreed to six. I also knew that we had agreed that this session was ideal in the progression toward a gold medal in the Mexico City Olympics, four months later. He said, 'I've got a wife and kids to get back to and we're over time already – just take the first step.' Something deep inside my befuddled brain said, 'Okay, I'll show him. I'll die! That will show him!'

I went out as hard as I could. I ran from the line like a madman, running flat out, with nothing left in the tank. By half way around it felt as if bits of my body were no longer attached to other bits that they should have been attached to. And no oxygen was getting to the parts that were supposed to be propelling me forward. The lack of co-ordination spread and flowing 2.5-metre strides dropped to 1 metre, my knees would not lift and my breath was starting to come out in groans. I reached the line and allowed my knees to sink to the track followed by the watery remains of the rest of my body. I lay face down, groaning out each breath, and I heard a giggle from Billy as he asked, 'Are you going to vote for me as the good guy of the year?' I had no energy to reply. I lay still for some minutes. It was some time before any life returned to my limbs, but it did, as it always does for an athlete in training. Eventually, Billy came back and in a mellow kind voice suggested that the next day I go for an easy run on the grass among the trees.

On the one hand, this session could be seen as cruel domination by an autocratic coach. However, from my side, it was the kindest gift he could have given to me at that stage in my preparation. If performers want to reach the top, there is no substitute for hard work. And it was my choice. His firmness was his gift to me. I would not have any Olympic medals without my two coaches, Fred Housden, my hurdles coach, and my undergraduate university coach, Billy, who taught me how to get more from myself when I did not think I could.

Billy and I had agreed on a specific number of laps that I wanted to complete (we agreed to six). Had he kept telling me to do, 'just one more' without discussion, there is no way that I would have completed the number I did in that session. Because we had made an agreement, I learned how many extra levels of capacity our bodies have.

It may seem that he lacked compassion, but that is to not understand the man. He cared so much that he had the courage to hold me to a promise and help me to exceed my own disbelief. In this case it was a physical stretch. In many other situations we may be able to help our young people through their mental disbelief. They may think they are not good enough. Our gift is to ask them first if they really want to achieve their goal, whether it be to learn to play the piano or to pass an exam well or to play for the team. Then we need to ask them what their first step is. And whether they would value our encouragement or support or even push, to take that first step. The first step is the most difficult.

■ Illustration of coaching a sports person by questioning

The following gives an illustration of what might be asked in a golf coaching session, although the activity could be anything. The key is to notice how the coach follows the performer's interest and that it is a process of personal discovery. Improvement comes from the young person's increase in self-awareness. Obviously input can come from the coach if the performer asks for it, but the point is to illustrate that our young people have much to contribute, as well as getting tips from us.

Coach: After your swing tell me what you noticed most. For example, what part did or didn't feel the way that you would want it to be?

Performer: What do you mean by that?

Coach: It might feel awkward or powerful, or whatever.

Performer (*after striking the ball*): It felt weak.

Coach: What part of it felt weak?

Performer: All of it!

Coach: Including the movement leading up to the contact?

Performer: Well no, kind of the result felt, sort of nothing.

Coach: What would you like it to be like?

Performer: I want to hit it cleanly and powerfully.

Coach: Which is more important to you to address first – cleanness or powerfulness?

Performer: Right now, power.

Coach: Okay. After your next swing, tell me where most of your power is coming from. Your upper half or lower half?

Performer (*after the swing*): Mostly from my arms.

Coach: Are you willing to look at all the areas that might be sources of power?

Performer: Sure.

Coach: Okay, would you give me a rating, on a 0–10 scale, of how much each part is involved in power on the next few swings? 10 means it is 100 per cent involved and used and 0 means none at all. What part would you like to start with?

Performer: I'll focus on my legs (*swings*). 3 or 4.

Coach: Would you be interested in holding your attention there and seeing what comes from each leg during your next swing?

Performer: Okay.

Coach: How happy are you with a 3–4 rating for your leg power involvement?

Performer: It's rubbish; I want at least a feeling of 8 to feel powerful.

Coach: I understand that you'd like to have higher scores in all areas, so that's a great overall personal performance objective. On each of these areas, I'm not asking you to try harder: in this case to use your legs more. I am simply asking you to observe what power comes from your legs this time – and then give that a rating.

The coach in this illustration is aiming to help the performer to explore a single focus on power, and notice its generation. As the young person pays attention to different parts, he or she will discover what is and is not contributing. As the young person discovers how little some areas are involved, their body will tend to use this information and will begin unconsciously to integrate it. The performer's task is to observe how much the power is increasing as focus is placed on each area. Their huge temptation is likely to be to attempt to direct power to that area and that then destroys the integrated swing. Clearly knowing and holding their intent on what they want, and then observing how close it comes to that, is an amazingly successful process. The mind moves the body, in synchronicity, towards the image it is holding. Therefore, the quality of the image held in the mind is critically important.

Valuable reminder: Often it can be useful to let the young person get on and practise. We don't need to bombard them continually with questions.

■ Learning and enjoyment

Sue Slocombe, who coached the British Olympic women's
hockey team, discovered that the less she told the young
performers, even at introductory level, the more they learned.
She let them experiment with how they held their hockey sticks
and in pairs immediately practise passing the ball. In the vast
majority of cases they found out for themselves where to place
their hands so that they were capable of hitting with more
power or more control.

Illustration of how to coach a group by questioning: by a
soccer coach:

Coach: Okay, what would you lot most want to work on today?

Group: (*Various suggestions.*)

Coach: Okay, I've heard some good ideas there. We've got a
game coming up, what are your views on what could be useful
drills and practice to prepare best for that?

Group: (*Again various thoughts offered.*)

Coach: Fine. I also have some areas I see as key. Let's split the
time and start with some of your ideas and we'll follow that
with the two more I believe are also critical to our success.

Now, you've mentioned keeping possession of the ball.
Obviously part of that is the quality of passing and another part
is timing, so you don't get caught or trapped in possession. On
the first of these I'd like you to pair up and pay attention to
what part of your foot strikes the ball on each pass. Also, where
on the ball did you make contact? I'd like you to tell your
partner exactly where you think contact was made on each and
what the result was. Ten minutes – let's go.

At the end of ten minutes the coach may ask the group for
feedback as to what they've noticed or learned.

The timing issue is one of awareness of self, partner and opposition positioning. The coach might ask them to notice exactly how far away an opponent needs to be to ensure that they have drawn them but far enough to avoid interception. The speed of pass will come into play here too. So the coach might set up some two-on-one drills and ask the two in possession of the ball to vary the distance between them and for the defender to help them with feedback as to when they felt committed to intercept but unable to get the ball. All of this is aiming to increase self and positional awareness.

■ Group training for individual sport

In individual sports but group activity, such as swimming or track and field athletics training, one or more of the following options might be used by a coach:

■ 'Part of the training today will focus on technique. I'd like you to do some accelerations and pay particular attention to your arms. Vary the angle a little and notice the effect it has.'

■ 'I'd like you to pay attention to your ankle motion. How much are your ankles moving through a complete range of motion?'

■ 'Where do you notice that most of your power is coming from? Ask yourself how much is coming from your upper half and how much from your lower half, to make 100 per cent. Come back and tell me what you noticed. By the way, there are no right answers here, just awareness of what works best for you.'

■ 'I'd like you to work on effort distribution. Notice the difference between 50, 60 and 70 per cent effort.'

Or, with a middle distance group:

■ 'We're going to work on pace judgment and I'd like each of you to lead one of the runs aiming to run each 200m in 32 seconds.

You can walk/jog the recovery 200m. But at the end of each repetition I'd like the leader to tell me the time they think they've hit before I tell you the time.'

■ The ideal would be to have the group involved in selecting some of the foci. As long as they are related to performance, learning and enjoyment, the results will improve.

■ Team success through involvement

Most of the illustrations used have been individually focused. The following was an early demonstration that involving a group or team through effective questions can be just as successful and powerful.

Joe Gough and the Field Gun Race

Back in 1990, I had a phone call from Joe Gough. He was the heavyweight boxing champion of the British armed services and with his looks and autocratic management style, his nickname was 'Blackbeard'. He had just become the Head Trainer for the Fleet Air Arm Field Gun Crew. A highly charged event was created in 1900 called the Field Gun Race. It was established to memorialise the heroic efforts of midshipmen who saved the lives of those in an encampment in southern Africa that was under siege. They did so by taking a cannon off their ship and running it over extraordinarily harsh terrain, including ravines and ridges. Because of their success in rescuing these men from certain death, the Field Gun Race was established to keep the memory alive. Each year at the Royal Tournament, until 2000, branches of the military services raced an old cannon with its tender and wheels over a course that represented the terrain and journey. The physical elite of the services would volunteer for these teams and being picked as a gunner was, for them, like being picked for the Olympic Games.

Every year they competed in matched pairs in afternoon and evening events, over a two-week period. They used the Earls

Court Arena; those who attended this spectacular saw the results of more than two months of intense training, as immense weights were moved at high speed, with awesome precision. (The barrel alone weighed over 400kgs and each wheel was over 40kgs.)

The course

Two teams at a time started from the middle of either side of the arena. Started by the noise of a flare exploding, each team of 16 men pulled their wheeled cannon and tender to the far end of the arena, turned it towards the centre and took it apart. They hoisted themselves and each part of the cannon over a 1.6m wall, then dragged it forwards and up a ramp of an imaginary chasm 7.5m wide. A rig and pulley system had to be lifted into place and anchored to the floor. Then one man would swing across and he and others would tow the remaining men and parts across. It took six trips to get all the men and all the machinery across. Two-thirds of the way down the arena they had to get all the men and parts through a hole in a second wall, which was just over 1 metre high, and just under 1 metre wide. The cannon and all constituent parts were put back together and towed to a line. When all 16 men were still, they had to fire three shells. The final time was taken as the third shell was fired. This was recorded and announced; then another charge was fired which signalled the start of the race back through the same course, taking down the rig and pulley and getting the reassembled cannon and all the men back over the start line.

How long do you think it took, given that the arena was about 80m long?

Some people have guessed 10 minutes and early on in training that would have been the time. However, the best time recorded for both directions combined was 2 minutes, 42 seconds! You had to see it to believe it was possible.

Asking how to win

Joe phoned and said that he had read the story of my positive/winning mental state vs. negative/losing mental-rehearsal exploits in my biography, *Another Hurdle*. He wanted to cover every possible base with his team and asked what I would be willing to do. I let him know that his impact on the team would be vital and invited him to come on a two-day questioning skills training course and to bring his Physical Training Instructors. To his great credit Joe came, and completely changed his highly autocratic style to one of involvement. He invited my colleague and course co-leader, Sir John Whitmore, and me to watch how he handled the training sessions. He was outstanding. He brought the team together after a run and had them sit down and would ask questions like, 'What happened that time?' or 'Where did anyone get slowed?' or 'Who blocked you and where were they going?' or 'The trainers say that this section was two seconds faster and that one a second slower; what happened in each of those areas?' 'Okay, let's walk through it, talk through it, look at the videos and tell me how it can be improved.' The awareness and ownership was shared by all of them.

The results?

For the first time in the 90-year history of the event Fleet Air Arm won every trophy – the 'A' Team, the 'B' Team, the fastest individual time, the aggregate time and the least penalty points. Added to that they had far fewer injuries than ever before. And perhaps the most significant of all was that they did that with 30 per cent fewer training runs than they had ever done before, meaning that they were truly working smarter, rather than just longer and harder.

What can we learn from this?

One key message is that the team members became more aware of their own processes and they took responsibility for what they would do to improve them. It does not mean that Joe abdicated responsibility. He felt just as much ownership of the outcome as they did but he was facilitating their development through increased personal involvement, mentally as well as physically; and no doubt at times making suggestions from his own years of experience.

You may have recognised that questions to groups or teams are rarely different from those you would ask of one individual.

The skill of the questioner is to facilitate thought and to request that those who speak infrequently have an opportunity to contribute – if they choose to do so.

■ Admitting mistakes

I drove down to the training base to congratulate the team and have a drink with them a few days after the event. One of the team members shared a learning point. He said that he found it interesting that the team members started to take ownership of their mistakes only after Joe had admitted he had made an error in judgment. He said that the team had trained all day and were asked to do another run and Joe went into his hut to make himself a coffee while they got set up. There was a belief in the team that another run was not going to help them. The equipment was so heavy and they were so tired that it would be counter-productive. They sent one of the Physical Training Instructors in to tell Joe, and waited with some apprehension to see how he would take this mutiny. Joe emerged to say that he heard what they were saying, that he would not force them to do another draining full run, but he would like them to re-run the hole in the wall before stowing their gear. The gunner telling this story said that it was a real turning point. They had been blaming others or making excuses for errors and from that point on there were apologies and personal acceptance of responsibility when they recognised that they had a lapse in concentration or missed timing or whatever.

The question that this raises is how often do we acknowledge and accept when we have made a mistake or an error of judgment? Our young people will learn that anyone can make a mistake and that an apology can come from any level. Initially we may feel quite challenged to apologise to a young person, but the positive impact that this can have, if it is accompanied by an explanation, can have great effect. Some adults are under the misapprehension that an apology is seen as a sign of weakness. Actually it can be exactly the opposite. You certainly win more hearts and minds by your honesty. If we try always to cover up, we may be seen as phoney or hypercritical. If they know that we are lying, the young people may take that example as their role model.

■ Generating feedback from the team

The following is an illustration of how we might use our questions to engage our young person's thinking when we want them to focus on a critical area for improvement. Let us assume that we have a young football team and they have demonstrated during the game that many of their passes are intercepted. Our closed and non-involving question might be, 'Would you like to do passing drills?' Our young people will probably say, 'Not much!'

Open questions can still get the young people to focus on the problem area, and at the same time these questions can make them think. Here is an illustration:

Coach: What was the primary cause of the problems for us in that game?

Players: We were feeling rushed. They were coming at us so fast.

Coach: What was the effect of you feeling rushed?

Players: It was difficult to control the ball.

Coach: Right. So if you were in a similar situation next time, what options would you have?

Players: Maybe we could pass sooner.

Coach: What would be the benefit of us doing some passing practice during our next session?

Players: Well, I suppose it might help us to get fewer interceptions in the next game.

Coach: Greater accuracy would help. How long shall we spend on that to give you a chance to feel in greater control under pressure; and what else would you like to practise?

What has the coach done in this example?

He or she has drawn from the players' recognition of the need to practise in a specific area. They have come up with their perception of why their performance was not great. They also have a better understanding of the benefit and need for this practice session. Why bother? Because they will have buy-in and more motivation as it came from them.

We may or may not get quite such useful feedback from our young people, but the main point of this illustration is that the adult has asked open questions that encourage the performers to engage and think about strategy and performance.

Using the right question

It bears repeating that 'what' is the most effective word with which to start most open questions. An infinite variety of words can follow that simple starter, and these will usually generate a fuller reply. It has been my experience over the last 15 years that at least 80 per cent of useful effective questions start with the word 'what'.

■ Feedback from an individual – listening with our heart as well as our head

Just suppose that our young person is playing in a hockey game. They have played really well for most of the game and we are proud of them. However, just before the finish they make a pass across the goal, an interception is made and our young person's team loses because of this action.

What do we say when they come off?

We have several choices. We could remain silent, in which case they might well assume that we are too angry or disappointed or full of blame to speak.

We could say, 'Well played,' and they could easily snap back, 'Didn't you see? I cost us the game!'

We could say, 'I'm really sorry that your last pass was intercepted.' He or she might say snidely, 'Terrific! I play well for 95 per cent of the game and all you can comment on is my one mistake!'

We could be in a no-win situation if we assume what they may need to hear. So we need to find a question that allows them to share their feelings or thoughts, when they are ready to do so. For example, 'When you feel like talking, I'd like to hear how you thought you played today, the good parts and things you can learn from.'

If the young person dwells on the negative, we can help them to acknowledge the reality, by asking questions that help to put it into perspective:

'What percentage of your game today were you happy with?'

'What do you need to do to come to terms with the disappointing part?'

'What did you learn from today, positives and negatives?'

'What would your team-mates want to hear from you?'

It does not mean that we do not bring in what we see as important. Just *start by asking their views* and once they have reasonably exhausted their list we can see whether there are still things that we believe are important to be raised at this time.

Measuring your response – when and how

It may well be best for the young person that we hold our observations or inputs until later. This can be hugely challenging for us. We may be dying to input and have to manage our own emotions. At this time, our self-regulation is both essential and demanding. Please do not take this as being an unemotional response. If we are excited and happy with an outcome, let us share our joy with them. It is when we are angry or hurt that our words come out inappropriately. We could be feeling let down or embarrassed. Something may slip out like, 'How could you have done that?' or 'It looked as if you just stopped trying!'

Look at the last two statements. We are making judgments and assumptions, and probably expressing them with an emotional charge. 'Poor me' or 'I need to let off steam!' is being felt and we will need a lot of maturity to step back and gauge what our young person needs most now. For example: even if they did give up, what was going on in their thoughts and feelings that caused that? What were they experiencing? How do they feel now? Would they do anything differently if they were in the same situation tomorrow? What would need to be different in them or their approach?

If we just cannot resist telling them what we feel or think, what will be the effect of that? There is a chance that they will remember any hurtful parts. Will they remember any significant learning points or will they want to reject any association with the situation? When they are under pressure again, will they really remember our words?

Challenging questions

A well-timed and probing question can help performers to shift out of their comfort zones, by their choice. During the Sydney Olympics, the British walker Chris Maddocks was seriously hurting from a pre-existing injury and was in last place out on the course in a 50km race. A couple of hours into the event he stopped at the side of the road to consult with a friend as to whether he should drop out. He was presented with a choice that provided an exceptional insight: 'Do you want to go on and hurt for a few hours after you finish or stop and hurt for the rest of your life?' Chris finished this, his fifth Olympics, to a standing ovation from 110,000 people.

Most of our decisions are not so dramatic, but each small step that carries our young people and us into the unknown can be a bit scary, awkward or uncomfortable. Our decisions may not always turn out to have been the right ones, but if we learn from what we experience we need not fear making a 'wrong' choice.

■ The power of alignment

Prior to the Sydney Olympic Games in 2000, I was reflecting on my experience in Mexico and realised that I had aligned my body, mind, emotion and spirit in my quest to get the best from myself in that Olympic Games. I decided to draft a letter to the athletes who were competing in the upcoming Games. I showed it to the Chief Executive of UK Athletics, Dave Moorcroft, who had established a world record over 5000m during his competitive career. Dave agreed that a copy should go to every member of our Olympic track and field team. The British Olympic Chef de Mission, Simon Clegg, also put it on the notice board in the Olympic Village, so that British Olympians from the other sports could read it.

14 August 2000

How to bring out your best in your competitions in Sydney

Dear [Athlete]

Congratulations on making the Olympic team. By now much of your hardest physical preparation is completed. And as you know, the closer you get to the time of your competition, the more your thoughts and emotions will play their part in how you do. Much has been written of the importance of clear, positive mental focus, and the need for your passion to empower your aims. Doing your best in the most important competitions of your life must be every performer's intent. What may be new is the thought that 'Only if an individual or team has a bigger mission or vision in mind will they lift themselves over the limits of self-interest.'

So how would a bigger mission help and what does it mean? Before answering that I'd like you to reflect on the development of humans. The sequence of conscious development is said to pass from body to mind to emotion to spirit. The last is often our search for meaning and purpose in our life. By aligning all parts of ourselves, with purpose and positive intent, we will be far more likely to fulfil our potential, in life and at the Games.

If you have not been asked the following aligning questions, then over the next few days or weeks, you might find them invaluable:

1 *What do I need to do physically to give myself the best chance of achieving my best in my competition in Sydney?*
2 *How positive, challenging, realistic and within my control is my aim?*
3 *How clearly have I thought through my possible strategies?*
4 *Where would be my best internal and external point of mental focus, at every moment of preparation and competition?*
5 *What would make my emotional passion, to do my best in this competition, a ten out of ten?*
6 *What could doing my best in these Games mean in life's bigger picture?*

The first five questions on body, mind and emotion may be familiar and are likely to have been covered by most top performers, but what of the spirit? Coming back to the question of lifting your performance, by having a higher purpose, let me ask you this: have you not already been asked to speak 'as an Olympian'?

Whether you like it or not, you are a role model for the next generation. For the sake of illustration, if you reach the top eight, or even becoming a medallist, it could mean some fame and some increased fortune, or at least a foot in the door for interviews for future work. This is great personally, and I hope that you reach your aims. Your life could also add value for others. Your performance could inspire others to achieve something special in their area of life.

The better you do at the Games, the more children's eyes will sparkle, and others will seek to hear your story and your messages. Fame and fortune can be fleeting, but your story can live on in the inspiration of others. So what is your story? You may have overcome injury or sickness; you may have overcome prejudice of gender, race, religion, class or education; you may have overcome a sense of inferiority or poverty; and you may want to share beliefs and ideas.

Simply, how could you be on a mission in the Games, one beyond the obvious self-interest? How can you link your intent to achieve with intent to serve?

Allow your true greatness to shine through your performance.

Very best wishes

David Hemery MBE, BSc, EdD
President UK Athletics

The reason for sharing this letter here is my belief that it has relevance to all our lives. Those heading to an Olympics were getting themselves ready for an intense self-challenge, at a fixed moment in time. It may not be an Olympic Games, but each of us has some personal challenges that will emerge in the future.

As Guardians, we have opportunities to be of service, to assist the development of our young people. Actions need to be aligned with this positive intent, if the best results are to be achieved.

The VEGA model

A powerful yet simple process can be used to help young people to sort out a meaningful direction for themselves. The process parallels my letter above and it is called VEGA. This stands for **Vision, Ethical values, Goals** and **Actions**. I experienced its power when my Olympic efforts had all these aligned.

V
I had a *Vision* that gave my aims a greater sense of meaning and purpose. A win could generate a platform to share inspirational thoughts and challenge others to fulfil their potential.

E

Ethical values have always been important to me – achieving without integrity lacks worth and is ultimately unsustainable, I believe. To race fairly, without drugs or psychological gamesmanship was vital to me.

G

My *Goal* was to run significantly under the World Record time and a strategy to achieve that end was discussed and agreed with both of my coaches.

A

My *Actions* involved total commitment of body, mind, emotion and spirit to fulfil that quest – to get the most out of my talent. The result was a 7m winning margin in a new world record.

■ Lack of Vision can result in false starts and costly misdirection.

■ Lack Ethical values and we can lose performers' hearts and minds and corrupt lives.

■ Lack Goals and we drift, lose energy and coherence of effort.

■ Lack Action and we generate nothing but inertia and frustration.

The mnemonic comes from one of my colleagues, and former schoolboy rugby international Les Duggan, with whom I work on leadership and alignment courses. He pointed out that Vega is the brightest star in the constellation of Lyra; and that, in ancient times, prior to the North Star being used, it was the guiding star for navigators. It seems appropriate that it can be a guiding star for our young people and for us.

Supporting young people to coach themselves

In his book *The Inner Games of Tennis*, Tim Gallwey said that the opponent in our head is often more daunting than the person on the other side of the net. We can be our own worst critic, saying things such as, 'I'll never be able to beat them!' or 'I bet they'll think I'm stupid!' or 'I'll never be able to learn this!' As Guardians of the Flame we need to help our young people to change their thinking from negative to positive. Can we help them to find an area over which they do have control and in which they can take a step forward?

Positive visualisation

As I have experienced myself, however effective, motivational and supportive the coaching, when an athlete or other sportsperson actually gets out on to the field or pitch in the moment of competition, they are on their own. It is possible in this time to become intimidated or alarmed by the situation, or by another athlete's abilities, and panic. As a coach it is important that we prepare our young person for these situations, by equipping them with the tools they need to meet the challenge and hold their nerve.

The point of sharing the following stories is to illustrate how I use my mind to change my state of apprehension or discomfort. What we can do as Guardians is to ask our young person to recall a time when they were feeling best able to cope with a similar situation.

How were they feeling?

How were they sounding?

How were they physically positioned?

How clear were they about their intent?

I had a special experience of the power of visualisation when I used it to help me to re-position my mind when panic hit in Mexico in 1968.

I was competing in the 400m hurdles in the 1968 Olympic Games. For me, the Olympic Games were a big 'end of term exam'. I wanted to do my best and I had prepared well. But so often we can lose all the benefit of that preparation in an instant, if we allow negative thoughts to overwhelm us and if we are not aware of our own reactions to a fear-producing situation.

I was warming up for the beginning of the race; I had finished jogging a couple of laps and sat down to put in my sprinting shoes. As I did so I faced the track and a rapid movement caught my attention. I saw Geoff Vanderstock, one of the favourites for my event, racing over the first 100m, including the first two hurdles. It appeared that he flew! So fast was his action that my heart hit my throat. 'He is in my event,' I thought, 'and I have to run faster than that!'

Self-awareness was the key. I recognised that my changed state of mind and my physical reaction had been caused by that vision of Geoff and were totally counterproductive to my performance. I could not control how fast he was capable of running. All I could do was to bring my own thoughts back under control, into the most positive mental state I could be in, in order to *do my best*. So I asked myself the question, 'When did you feel totally in control, strong, fast and happy?'

The answer was: near to the start of this Olympic preparation year, fourteen months earlier, with the warm autumn sun on my back, running on firm sand at the edge of the water, along Powder Point, near Duxbury, Massachusetts. That peninsular extends along 5km of golden sand. I was alone, striding, lifting my knees so that each footfall was landing in about 15cms of water on the edge of the surf. I had accelerated to a speed that would have been a good 4×400m relay pace, gliding, floating and flying down a back straight. It felt fluid, fast and exhilarating. After what seemed like ages I was not feeling tired, so I picked up the pace even more and held that for what seemed like endless time. The sensation was one of pure joy.

So here, in the Olympic arena, I decided to take myself back to that time. I removed my shoes and socks and jogged forward on to the infield, where the grass was still damp from the afternoon rain. It allowed me to relive the feeling of the water under my feet. I did not try to run very fast, but to just glide, simply putting myself back into the state of being in control, within the joyful feeling of fluid movement. It took less than two minutes but the transformation of feeling and mental state was total: from weak to strong, from tense to relaxed, from anxious to confident.

When our young people are aware of feeling panic or of being out of control, we can ask them to recall a time when they were performing at their best, feeling confident, powerful and relaxed, or whatever state they need to be in to perform well. If we can draw that from them, then whenever they are starting to feel out of control or out of their comfort zone, they can mentally revisit the time and emotional state when they were well prepared to do their best.

Self-questioning, to bring out our best

Having considered the effectiveness of coaching-by-questioning, we need to consider how we can pass on some of that power to the young person themselves, and enable them to ask themselves questions which will help them to improve their performance and achieve their goals.

As discussed before, the coach–sportsperson relationship is a partnership. Often it is part of our coaching responsibility to monitor our young person's progress and ability. Gaining their agreement in coaching sessions – as my coach, Billy Smith, did with me – on the goals they want to achieve, and how they feel during their practice sessions, can inspire a deeper commitment from them to keep pushing themselves.

The questioning technique is one which helps us, as coaches, to monitor what they want and how they are managing and feeling – physically and emotionally.

As discussed, an effective method is to ask your young person to use a scale of 1-10 to help recognise and choose to extend their self-imposed limits.

Here is how I used this self-questioning during a training run in the winter of 1971-72, while I was studying at Harvard University.

I was aiming to set a personal best on a 16km run along the riverbank path and over two bridges. At about 11km I felt the urge to slow down. Before doing so, I used some self-coaching questions. The first was to ask myself, 'What has sent that message to slow down?' I checked various parts of my body. My legs felt fine, my arms were okay, but when I paid attention to my abdomen, I suddenly realised, 'Here's the problem.' I had been breathing heavily for nearly forty minutes and I was feeling quite a strong discomfort where my chest had been heaving oxygen in and out, at a higher rate than usual. Again, without breaking stride, I asked myself, 'On a scale of 1-10, if 10 would put you in hospital, what's it on now?' I rated it a 7. I then asked myself, 'What number would you be willing to live with, on this run, in order to ensure a new personal best time?' I thought, 'I *could* live with a 9.'

So I kept up the pace of my running and started to monitor the discomfort level, at each new benchmark. By the next clump of trees, a few hundred metres further on, it was up to 7.1. By the next bench on the path, it was 7.2. I kept this up all the way to the finish of the run, and as I raced through the door, stopping my watch in a new best time for that route, the discomfort rating was up to 7.8. I was sweating profusely. My chest was heaving *and* I had a big grin on my face, thinking - wow! I could have kept that up for another kilometre!

Obviously this was a chosen discomfort and I was in control, but I am absolutely certain that I would have slowed down if I had not been through that self-monitoring process. It has stood me in good stead in other areas of my life since. It is such a simple and yet effective tool.

One natural outcome of using this technique with the young people we support is that they will learn naturally to self-monitor, and take on personal responsibility to choose their own levels of ability and comfort and assess what is acceptable as well as possible in moving their limits back – extending their comfort zones.

Before backing off from any endeavour, we should encourage them to ask themselves:

'What sent the message?'

'What triggered the desire to stop?'

They may have to check their body, mind, emotion and spirit to see *where* the primary discomfort is centred, or from where it is emanating.

Once the origin has been identified, it is worth asking:
'On a scale of 1-10: what is the discomfort rating?'
Then ask:
'Is this just gradual discomfort or is it a genuine health warning?'

This is a $10 million question. *Most* of the time it is likely to be discomfort. Apart from checking with a medical person, I have no specific guidelines for deciding between over- and under-caution. I would suggest that we encourage our young people to increase their self-awareness, so that the telltale signs of needing to back off are heeded.

If they assess that it is fine to push on, then encourage them to ask, 'What could I tolerate in this situation?' Usually this number is higher than the current reality score. They should continue monitoring: 'What's it on now?', 'How willing am I to hang on while hurting?' They may even want to compare themselves with their mates or others, thinking, 'I bet they wouldn't be willing to hang on like this.' This is part of building self-confidence, if they believe that they are working harder than others.

We must use commonsense caution around injury – psychological or physical. We also need to recognise that suggesting that they should stop may be similar to a parent saying, 'You're going to fall!' to their child. We do not want to project limitations, and we do not want to be pushing and uncaring or cause damage. This is why we need them to develop ever-increasing personal awareness and responsibility – finding their own inner authority. The mind normally sends out 'caution' messages, to give us time to think and decide whether it is okay to press on. Extending our personal limits is a victory largely for our conscious mind. It is important to remind ourselves that the body *adapts during recovery time*. That means asking our young people to monitor their recovery and to take sufficient recovery after intense activity.

Some people need only a set of guideline questions to self-coach. This doesn't work for everyone, however, and it may also remove the control slightly further away from the young person. It may be helpful for them to develop their own self-questions. But here are a few 'thought starters' as examples:

■ 'If we were advising someone who was going to question us, what would we suggest they ask?'

■ 'Where should they be probing and challenging to get the best out of us?'

■ 'What should they be asking to assist our clarity?'

■ 'How tough would we want them to be and in what areas? For example, extending our comfort zones.'

■ 'What degree of pressure gets the best from us? For example, being clear on time targets and deadlines.'

■ 'What would be the most fruitful area to dig – to get the most from us?'

The young person can look at these questions and think to themselves: 'I can answer these questions, because they force me to look at myself, and my situation, with a degree of detachment.'

Reflective questions can help young people to sort out their priorities in the use of time and the best focus of their attention at any moment. Coaching which not only uses questioning techniques, but also tries to pass on some of those techniques to the young person, should help them to achieve more, and more and with safety. In teaching our young people to answer questions they pose to themselves, we can launch them on to further and ever more adventurous paths.

Self-healing

Another way in which adults can have a very powerful influence on the capacity of young people to take personal responsibility is to encourage them to look after their health.

In an experiment in the USA, some young people with cancer were asked to imagine that their white blood cells could act as knights in armour, attacking their tumours. They were x-rayed before and after this process and, in many cases, there were significant reductions in the size of their tumours. Do we take sufficient responsibility for our health? What questions could we ask our young people, as well as ourselves, to become more responsible?

I had an interesting personal experience of self-healing advice in 1985. I had developed a bone spur (calcification) on my right heel. My Achilles tendon became so sore as a result that I could not bear the pressure of my shoe against it. I decided to consult my doctor. He sent me to a specialist, who x-rayed it and told me that I had two options. I could have an operation and would have a 50 per cent chance of running again, or I could just stop running! Neither choice sounded good. Running is not for everyone, but for me it has been hugely enjoyable and also provided a balance in my life. I went home feeling seriously depressed.

Coincidentally my wife had seen a card in a local shop that afternoon for Alex Sautelle, an osteopath and naturopath who was practising locally at the time. He has since qualified as a medical doctor and general practitioner. He told me to do stretching exercises, put my foot alternately in buckets of hot and cold water and, in his medical room, I sat my heel on a magnetic pad. During the course of consulting, I made note of some interesting books in his room. We explored some shared beliefs and, seeing that I was open-minded, he told me he believed that the mind can influence matter. He suggested that I imagine the spur dissolving, and then to imagine my heel in the healthy shape that I would like it to be. I did this half a dozen times in the next couple of weeks, while continuing the treatment.

I went back to see him a few weeks later and during the course of the examination he stopped to check, 'Which heel is it?' I have not had a single day off from heel pain since, and that was twenty years ago.

I use this story to illustrate that there are more options available to us than the conventional wisdom of the day might suggest, especially if we are willing to take personal responsibility. Have we taken inner authority away from our young people? What can we do to redress this?

Relieving headaches

Don't ask me how this works. All I know is that it does in most cases. When a child complains of a headache, ask them to close their eyes and tell you what size it is and what colour it is. You might ask whether it is the size of a basketball or a grapefruit or a tennis ball? When they have told you what it's like, ask them to imagine it turning to liquid and allow it to pour into an imaginary bucket in front of them. After a short while ask them to let you know when that has finished. Sometimes the headache goes after the first visualisation. The child will normally open their eyes and say, 'Okay, I've done that.' Then ask them to close their eyes again and tell you what size and colour the headache is now. Usually the size is smaller and the colour lighter. Simply ask them to repeat the process, as many times as needed. Usually the headaches disappear or are dramatically reduced.

Pain relief

Children often hurt themselves. You can help them to help themselves by asking them to take a deep breath and imagine themselves breathing into the area of pain. This can have a great relieving effect. If an area aches, another technique is to imagine a warmth flowing into the area of discomfort.

The benefits of generating self-challenges

I have had the chance to see the responses and benefits of measuring self-challenges in three different age groups. Whilst teaching at Millfield School in Somerset, I looked after a remedial weight-training group. This group included a few young people, one of whom could not do a single sit-up and several who could not manage one press-up. One young lad in the latter group started with a 7kg bar that he would try to push up while lying on a bench with no added weights at all. He managed three repetitions initially. This set his benchmark and he progressed from there. Via this process, each child established their own reality and their own self-targets from which they would aim to improve. The group soon gathered around and supported each other's efforts to reach five, eight or ten repetitions the next week. The mutual support and enthusiasm generated rapid and vast improvements. These were recorded. The mutual recognition, increased self-belief and the sense of self-worth were infectious. There was a real buzz in the class – the young people were enjoying it and improving greatly. Their motivation was coming from within.

The second group was at Boston University where I was head track coach. At the first cross-country meet following my appointment our team finished fifth of five, by a considerable margin. In order to give them a realistic goal to strive for I put their personal running times on the notice board and asked the question, 'By how much can you beat your time over the same distance next week?' Their improvement in the following week's race ranged from about 20 seconds to one and a half minutes, over 8km. The comments and congratulations came as much from their peers as from me. Their success bred more success and their self-confidence rose weekly. These athletes continued to improve and some new recruits with more natural ability, who could challenge for the lead, joined them. The combination of the two approaches soon helped to develop a winning team, as well as highly motivated personal successes.

The third group were aged eight to eleven and at a Saturday morning athletics club started by my wife and me. We did virtually no skills training, but simply told the children the rules and asked them to give things a try. In the second week, three of the group wanted to run 200m; but one small girl came up to the line, looked over at the girl next to her and then stepped back, saying, 'Oh, I don't want to run against her, she's too fast!' My reply was along the lines of, 'Oh, never mind how fast she runs. See if you can beat the time you did last week, which was...' She grinned and happily came up to the line, dashing away on the word 'go'. When she finished with a 1.5-second improvement, I congratulated her with genuine enthusiasm in my voice. She gave a little scream of delight and ran over to share her achievement with her friend.

Some of the parents of those children said to us, 'We don't know what you're doing, but the children are waking us early on Saturday mornings, to ensure we're ready to bring them here by 9.30. They can't wait to get here and they're loving it.'

The essential ingredients in all these illustrations are *measurement* and *recognition*. It really is that simple. Recognition, for effort and personal improvement, can often be far more rewarding than something material. Most professional sports stars are more interested in achieving a title than the income. Of course, the prize money is important, especially in the early days, but in the long run it is the recognition that counts.

As adults our questions need to generate enthusiasm and assist our young people in the building of self-belief, to help them to set realistic and challenging targets and then support and challenge them in their achievement. As well as asking them how they believe they have done against their goals, we need to follow up by acknowledging and praising their genuine efforts and achievements.

5

General questioning techniques

The art of asking questions

The Nobel Prize-winning physicist Isidor Isaac Rabi, who invented a method of probing the structure of atoms and molecules in the 1930s, attributed his success to the way his mother used to greet him when he came home from school each day: 'Did you ask any good questions today?'

This approach differs considerably from the normal concerned parent who asks how the day was, or 'Did you learn anything new today?' For me, Rabi's experience is striking, because his mum was asking him to think beyond what he was being told; to be willing to challenge his own as well as his teachers' thinking.

Can we imagine asking our young people to start asking us questions? We get bombarded when they are very young and many of us get so fed up we try to suppress their sense of inquiry. In doing this, we may well dull much of their natural curiosity and enthusiasm for learning.

■ Open, closed and leading questions

Questioning is such a crucial skill – there are various different kinds, and we need to learn to use them in the most appropriate contexts. The two most obvious question types are perhaps 'closed' and 'open' questions. So what are the effects and uses of open and closed questions?

Most of the time, closed questions and leading questions are unhelpful to the development of our young people. A closed question produces a yes/no or single-word answer. A leading question has our own content and intent in it, such as:

'Don't you think it's a good idea for you to start your homework as soon as you get home from school?'

Both closed and leading questions are used when we are on our agenda and doing the thinking for our young person. The effect of doing the thinking for them is that we fail to 'grow' our young people. Most closed questions start with a verb, and our idea or our focus is in our question:

'Have you practised hard enough this week?'

'Will you go to bed now?'

'Have you done your homework?'

'Did you do your piano practice?'

'Do you know when the bus is leaving?'

None of the above generate self-awareness or self-responsibility.

Questions that can help to move forward on any issue

Using GROW

GROW is outlined on page 84. It is a sequence used by thousands of people to help with decision-making. It may not be necessary always to go through a long coaching session. Single open questions that provoke thought are often valuable, such as: 'What do you think is our best next step on this project?' However, if the issue is one on which it may be useful to spend some time, this sequence can be invaluable.

Below, I outline the intent and focus of each of the four areas of questioning and include a list of sample questions. This should not be used as an interrogation. Ideally, the questions form part of a coaching conversation, in which our aim is simply to help the young person become more aware of what they want, what is happening in their situation, what they could do about it and then to choose to take responsibility for taking their next step to move the issue forward.

G

The G in the GROW sequence stands for *Goal*. Perhaps our greatest gift in our conversation with the young person is to help them to clarify what they really want. It will assist them if they phrase their goal, aim or interest in positive language. That means that they state what they do want, rather than what they do not want or would like to avoid. For example, 'I don't want to fail this exam' can be restated as 'I want to aim for a passing grade.' 'I don't want to be late' can become 'I'd like to be there at least five minutes before the start time.'

It will help the focus of the conversation if, right up front, we get them to tell us what they would like to have by the end of our conversation with them. It might be to have greater clarity; it could be that they want some new ideas or options; or they may want to make a decision. It is an invaluable guide for us to have the young person say what they want from their discussion with us. This could be referred to as the goal of the discussion. Additional questions are needed to establish their goal for their issue.

Sample questions:

■ 'What would you like to get from our discussion on this issue?'

■ 'What do you really want?' (Make sure that their aims are worded positively.)

■ 'If you got that, what will it give you?'

■ 'What control or influence do you have over this goal/aim?'

■ 'By when do you want to achieve your goal?'

■ 'What would be a step on the way?'

■ 'When do you want to achieve this by?'

■ 'Is your aim sufficiently challenging to be motivating for you?'

■ 'What needs to be in it to make it really worthwhile for you?'

■ 'How attainable is this?'

■ 'How will you measure or assess your success?'

Once sufficient time has been given to discussion around what they really want, the second area is to help the young person to clarify what is really going on. Most people will look at a situation from their own perspective. One thing we can do with our questions is to shift and expand the young person's view and understanding. For example, we might ask what effect the issue is having on the others involved. We may ask how big an issue it is.

R

The R in GROW stands for *Reality*. Why should we bother to explore this? Sometimes the issue a young person begins with is different from the underlying issue. For example: 'I hate physical education' may have a wide variety of possible underlying issues. It could be embarrassment with changing in front of peers. It might be that they consider themselves poor at an activity. Or it might be any of a number of other factors.

Our questions need to allow the person to see their issue either more deeply or from another perspective. This may involve us challenging some phrases, such as 'No one likes me' or 'I never get picked to play.' A simple starting comment might be: 'Tell me more' and then to listen. Our challenge is to enable young people to make discoveries and insights for themselves.

Sample questions:

- 'What is happening at the moment regarding this issue?'

- 'When does it happen? Where is it happening? How often is it happening?'

- 'How much of an issue is it for you?'

- 'Who is involved – directly and indirectly?'

- 'When things are not going well on this issue, what is the effect on you?'

■ 'What happens to the others directly involved?'

■ 'What or who else gets affected?'

■ 'What have you done so far to move this forward?'

■ 'What results did this produce?'

■ 'What's missing in the situation?' (For example: clarity, trust, support, understanding, time, finance?)

■ 'What resources or people do you have that you are not using?'

■ 'What is holding you back?'

Try using your intuition to see what is really going on. (Beneath many issues are others, such as power and control issues, or lack of confidence.)

O

The O in GROW stands for *Options*. Once the reality and goal are more clearly understood, the third area of questioning is concerned with looking for possible solutions. It is valuable to recognise that often there is more than one solution. Even if a reasonable suggestion comes up early, there is often benefit in drawing out a wider spectrum of possible solutions.If the young person is old enough to write, it can be very useful if they are asked to take note of all the possible ways forward. Having them, rather than us, do the writing is important for the sake of their ownership. The options will be in their words and they are the ones who must take responsibility for what they will do.Tempting as it is, as adults we need to keep our ideas back until after the young person has dried up, otherwise they can lose ownership of their thoughts. I have found that if the temptation to share my ideas early on in the conversation feels overwhelming, it is useful to make a discreet note of a trigger word or two, just so that I do not forget the ideas. I can then continue to listen fully to what they are saying without being distracted by my own thoughts or interrupting their flow.

Sample questions:

- 'What options do you have?'

- 'What could you do?'

- 'What else could you do?' (*This can be asked several times – until no new options come up.*)

- 'From whom might you seek advice?'

- 'Who has handled this sort of problem really well? What have they done that you might try?'

- 'What if…?' (*These can be as creative as we make them. The aim is to break the young person out of their limited thinking, that they are too small, or too weak, or too stupid.*)

- '… you had unlimited time to give to this issue, what would you do then?'

- '… you had even less time but had to do something, what might you try?'

- '… you had unlimited money to focus only on this issue, how would you use it to move the issue forward?'

- '… you had the power, authority or complete autonomy to do what you wanted, what would you do?'

- '… you had a magic wand? What would you most want to change and to what?'

- '… you had a really wise old friend, who knew you and this situation really well; what advice would they be giving you?'

- '… a friend of yours had this issue, what advice would you be giving them?'

■ 'Knowing what you know now, if you could have a fresh start, what would you do?'

■ 'What quality in yourself, if it were enhanced, would most help your situation?' (For example, confidence, tolerance.)

If we have other ideas we can ask:

■ 'Would you like a suggestion?'

W

The W in GROW stands for *Will*. The last part of the conversation is important in order for the young person to know exactly what they are agreeing to do. What are they willing to do in order to move their issue forward? It does not matter if their next step is not very large, as long as it is forward and they are committed to taking it. Occasionally, it may be appropriate to agree to wait and take no step until the situation has evolved some more. In this case, we should agree a time when they will review the situation.

Will questions differ from those in the first three areas. Clarifying the Goal, the Reality and the Options are all concerned with raising awareness. The Will section is about generating the young person's responsibility, by asking them to make a choice and commit to doing something to move their issue forward.

Sample questions:

■ 'Which option or options will you choose to take forward?'

■ 'To what extent will this meet your goal, objective or aim?'

■ 'When precisely are you going to start and aim to finish each agreed step?'

■ 'What could get in the way and how will you ensure that it doesn't?'

■ 'What will help to ensure that you will do what you are saying?'

■ 'Who needs to know that you are planning to do this?'

■ 'What support do you need and from whom?'

■ 'How will you get that support?'

■ 'What could I do to support you?'

■ 'How committed are you to this first step?'

■ 'How clear are you about what the first step is?' (*Sometimes the first step may be to speak with someone, or it may be to give careful thought to what is going to be said and perhaps even sound out someone to hear whether the intent comes across in the way the young person wants.*)

The questions outlined in the four GROW sections above can be used to help move forward on any issue. You may need to alter the wording in a way that feels comfortable and conversational for you. In all cases, keep the questions short and well focused.

■ Clarifying commitment – the three steps

Sometimes a conversation may finish with what we believe to be a good outcome only to find that the young person rates their commitment to action step quite low..The first thing to check is that they are rating their willingness to take their action step, rather than the likelihood of its success.

If they are still giving a low score, and if the action step is within their control, there are only three areas that could be blocking them.

Step 1

The first step takes place in the mind: this is the thought level.

■ How clear are they about their step?

■ If it is not totally clear, what further clarification is needed? Another mental check is whether this is really a priority for them. Your questions are aimed to help them to clarify their thoughts.

Step 2

The second area is their feelings: this step takes place at the emotional level.

■ How high or low is their confidence or enthusiasm for the action? Again our questions need to ask the young person what he or she needs to increase confidence or enthusiasm to get on with the first step.

Step 3

The third and final area that might block action is their will:

■ Do they really have the intent, commitment and willingness to take an action step?

■ What will help them to overcome their inertia?

The statement to summarise these three steps is: *'Align their Thought, Feeling and Will into their Action!'* Easier to remember is: *'Align their Head, Heart and Guts into their Action.'*

■ Summary of key hints and tips for questioners

■ Keep questions short, simple and succinct, and avoid asking more than one question at a time.

■ Primarily ask questions that the performer can answer from their experience.

■ Start most questions with 'What…'

■ Largely avoid 'Why' questions, as they can put people on the defensive, and into analysis rather than increased awareness.

■ Give the young person time to think and reply, before you add another question.

■ Use closed questions to focus in. For example, 'Is that a priority for you?' then broaden again to, 'What else?'

■ Notice which questions produce good results for you.

■ Practise questioning with a friend, so you understand your own response to effective and less effective questioning.

■ Become comfortable with not knowing where the conversation or outcome may go.

■ Selflessness is a key attribute of a good questioner. A big challenge is to hold back from telling young people *our* story or our preferred solutions for them.

■ Can we listen with our hearts? Research has discovered that there are about a million neurons around the heart and the gut, as well as those in the brain. This helps to validate listening to 'gut feelings' about a right course of action or whether to trust someone. By opening our heart when listening to our young people, we can increase our ability to relate in a way that is powerful and will help to grow their potential.

Epilogue

How do we sustain change?

We need reminders. These will be different for each of us. But here are a few thought starters. We could:

- Ask a friend to monitor our 'telling' before we 'ask', and let us know when we slip back into it.

- Let our young people know our aim is to ask/involve them and their ideas more, and ask them for feedback.

- Place reminder notes in strategic places – 'What effective questions did I ask today?'

- Give ourselves rewards for our attempts and remembering.

- Avoid beating ourselves up; just monitor learning (if we recognise that we have missed an opportunity, at least we are aware of it and that is the first step).

- Practise with a friend, asking questions of them and really listening to their issues, rather than providing solutions as our first intervention.

- Practise on ourselves – asking self-awareness questions.

- Practise listening more with our heart: beyond the words, what message comes from their eyes, or their tone of voice; or ask what prompted a frown or a head shake.

- Find specific opportunities to practise the skills. Practice is key.

- Monitor each day: how often in everyday life do you use questioning for awareness in others?

- Review progress.

If some of the cartoons, stories or ideas in this book have raised your awareness of the need to do something differently, my hope is that you will act.

I would like to close this text with three quotations that I have used often at the close of my business coaching courses:

The first comes from the late eighteenth-century Irish philosopher and politician, Edmund Burke:

No man ever made a greater mistake than to do nothing, when he could only do a little.

If we all did a little more effective asking and listening, there could be a huge change in the attitude and enthusiasm of our young people.

The second quotation is from Anita Roddick, founder of the Body Shop:

If you think you're too small to make a difference, you've obviously never been in bed with a mosquito!

In working with young people, this says to me that any of us can have a great impact. We may not know it at the time, but if we truly care about supporting and making a difference, the smallest amount of time given or the simplest kind word may bring change.

The final quotation comes from Abraham Maslow, the psychologist, who used to gather his first-year university students together, on their first day, and ask them:

Which of you is going to become great in your chosen field? If not you, who then? Why not you?

And later was added:

If not now, when?

I would like to leave you with a similar challenge, in becoming great Guardians of the Flame. I cannot think of a more important quest than to develop the potential of the next generation. I wish you well in that essential and positive endeavour.

Acknowledgements

There are probably hundreds of people to whom I owe acknowledgments, not least the educators such as Chris Argyris, Tim Gallwey, Daniel Goleman, Abraham Maslow and Carl Rogers. Others who have helped my thinking and given practical advice are: Jonathan Brown, for reading and practical suggestions; Les Duggan, my business partner in Developing Potential Ltd, a highly supportive colleague and friend for multiple readings and recommendations; Richard Evans; Richard Handover, for articulating the need for a cartoon emphasis; Gillian Hill, for some exceptional assistance with editing comments; my family – Adrian, Peter and V Hemery – from whom I have received much inspiration; David Lewis, the creative and gifted cartoonist; Chris Loe; Emma Shackleton, Commissioning Editor, BBC Worldwide, for her open-minded and enthusiastic support for this book; Sarah Sutton and Ruth Baldwin for their fine editorial work; Bob Thompson, for reading and supportive comments; Bruce Tulloh; and David Whitaker and John Whitmore, my founding coaching colleagues. I am deeply grateful to you all.

Key word index